*Fictional Worlds*

# Fictional Worlds

Thomas G. Pavel

Harvard University Press
Cambridge, Massachusetts,
and London, England 1986

*Library of Congress Cataloging-in-Publication Data*

Pavel, Thomas G., 1941–
  Fictional worlds.

  Bibliography: p.
  Includes index.
  1. Fiction.   2. Semantics.   I. Title.
PN3331.P36   1986        801.'953        86-299
ISBN 0-674-29965-5 (alk. paper)

*For Mihai*

# Preface

THE LAST few decades have witnessed a considerable variety of research on narrative and dramatic fiction focused on the formal properties of literary texts. The semantics of fiction has remained, however, at the periphery of critical attention. Yet a comprehensive theory of literature needs a viable account of literary content that would complement formal and rhetorical studies. In contrast to the reluctance of formalist poetics to address the semantic aspects of fiction, recent analytical philosophy and aesthetics have been devoting an ever-increasing energy to their exploration. The temptation to cross boundaries soon became irresistible, and indeed most literary scholars who offer semantic contributions have borrowed their notions from modal logic and speech-act theory.

By proposing a survey of the semantics of fiction, I am attempting to pave the way for a theory sensitive to the nature and function of imaginary worlds, the representational force of fiction, and the links between literature and other cultural systems. After an introduction that criticizes classical structuralism, Chapters 2 and 3 evaluate the literary relevance of various philosophical stands on fictional beings and worlds. An exploration, in the fourth chapter, of several features of fictional worlds leads, in Chapter 5, to a discussion of literary conventions. The links between fiction and the broader economy of culture constitute my last chapter.

Earlier versions of parts of this book appeared in the following journals, and I am grateful for permission to reuse the material: *Journal of Aesthetics and Art Criticism* for "Possible Worlds in Literary Semantics" (1975) and "Ontological Issues in Poetics" (1981); *Poetics* (North-Holland Publishing Company, Amsterdam) for "Fiction and the Causal Theory of Names" (1979) and "Tragedy and the Sacred" (1982); *Studies in 20th Century Literature* for "Fictional Landscapes" (1982); *Philosophy and Literature* for "Incomplete Worlds, Ritual Emotions" (1982); and *Poetics Today* for "Borders of Fiction" (1983).

I wish to express my gratitude to the Social Science and Humanities Research Council of Canada, for several research grants, and to the Canada Council for the Killam Research Fellowship, which enabled me to spend 1980–81 at Harvard University and 1982–83 at the Ecole des Hautes Etudes en Sciences Sociales, Paris, where I finished the first draft of this book. I am grateful to the University of Quebec at Montreal for secretarial help during the last stages of manuscript preparation.

A large number of colleagues, students, and friends offered stimulating criticism and advice. Special thanks are due to Keith Arnold, Morton Bloomfield, Claude Bremond, Christine Brooke-Rose, Lubomir Doležel, Umberto Eco, Wlad Godzich, Claudio Guillen, Benjamin Hrushovski, Jens Ihwe, Zoltan Kanyo, Shalom Lappin, Georges Leroux, Brian McHale, Dan Nescher, Hilary Putnam, Marie-Laure Ryan, Teun van Dijk, Douglas Walker, and John Woods.

I feel particularly indebted to Menahem Brinker and Kendall Walton, whose detailed remarks and suggestions have been included in the present version. Warm thanks go to my editors, Joyce Backman and Lindsay Waters, for their good advice and unfailing patience.

# Contents

*Fictional Worlds*

# 1 ~ Beyond Structuralism

M Y purpose in this book is to discuss some of the main issues raised by the theory of fiction, a field emerging at the crossroads of literary criticism and philosophy. On the philosophers' side, the interest in fiction fits naturally into the development of modern philosophies of language and logic. Starting with Frege, Russell, and Wittgenstein, the program of analytical philosophy had as its central task the clarification of philosophical language through careful scrutiny of concepts and the construction of powerful logical models. During the early stages of the inquiry, philosophers focused their attention on freeing rational discourse from the trappings of ordinary, prelogical language, wherein vague, ambiguous expressions often display a linguistic form quite at variance with their logical structure, sometimes misleadingly referring to nonexistent entities. Regimentation of language involved the elimination of ambiguities and of misguided reference; it therefore had to devote considerable energy to forging a secure link between linguistic expressions and the states of affairs talked about, between language and reality. But since, within the language of unmistakable truth, expressions such as "the flying bird" and "the flying horse" receive a different treatment (the first expression readily accepted, the second failing referential tests), philosophers were inevitably led to favor literal varieties of language over fictional and metaphoric uses. The logical formalisms proposed during this period expressly eliminated fictional language as a deviant phenomenon that hinders the course of representational language.

More recently, however, as the earlier self-righteousness and reformatory intentions of analytical philosophy gradually gave way to an outlook more tolerant of the variety of linguistic uses, philosophers of logic and language started to question the soundness of limiting the inquiry to plain referential discourse. The reorientation brought about by research in modal logic and possible-world semantics has drawn the attention of logicians toward the close kinship between possibility and fiction: formerly underrated, fiction begins to serve as a means of checking the explanatory power of logical hypotheses and models. Since fictional discourse allows for any imaginable kind of confabulation without constraint, and since the rebellious properties of literary and mythological fiction challenge most models and appear to defy easy regimentation, literary phenomena may be understood to provide a severe testing ground for formal semantics.[1]

Outside logic proper, the more relaxed standards of analytical philosophy have led to a revival of concern for the properties of fiction: aiming at prospecting the entire spectrum of linguistic activities, speech-act philosophers cannot neglect fictional discourse, while tolerant epistemologists, replacing the classical idea of a reality unique and undivided with a multiplicity of equally valid world versions, have come to look at fiction as just another of these numerous versions, by no means less worthy than its competitors.[2]

### Structuralism and Literary Semantics

In literary criticism and theory, the growing interest in the properties of fictional discourse grew during a period when structuralist methods and ideas increasingly met with challenge. Not unlike the early opponents of structuralism, who disliked the invasion of a scientific ideology into the private grounds of the humanities, poststructuralist and deconstructionist critics reacted against structuralism's taste for sciencelike certitudes. To the quest for a unique, well-defined structure of the literary text, the poststructuralists contrasted the search for multiple readings, destined to show that there is no such thing as *the* meaning or *the* structure of a work.[3] In a similar vein, although from a different angle, various trends in reader-oriented criticism denounced the structuralist obsession with objective properties of the literary text, showing that it inevitably led to the neglect of reception processes (Suleiman, 1980; Tompkins, 1980).

But impatience with structuralist scientific pretentions, or with the unremitting search for objective and universal literary properties, is not the only conceivable reaction to this trend. Opposition to structuralism just may as well originate in the feeling that while its strongly advertised call for a rational, scientific study of literature was indeed worth pursuing, the structuralist way of implementing its own program most often failed to do justice to the expectations raised.

In a series of influential papers that laid the foundation of French structuralism, Claude Lévi-Strauss summoned anthropology and more generally the humanities to reach for a new scientific status by emulating the advances of structural linguistics and more specifically by applying phonological models, which in his view represented the paradigm of scientific success in a social field. Claiming that earlier mythological research failed to understand the arbitrariness of linguistic signs, he submitted that since myths behave like a language, to miss this essential truth amounted to being blocked at a prescientific stage. For him, arbitrariness freed mythological meaning from its dependence on the superficial features of given stories or story schemata. Carl Jung's assumption that a given mythological pattern always has the same meaning "is comparable," Lévi-Strauss wrote, "to the long supported error that a sound may possess a certain affinity with a meaning: for instance the 'liquid' semivowels with water . . . Whatever emendation the original formulation may now call for, everybody will agree that the Saussurean principle of the *arbitrary character of the linguistic sign* was a prerequisite for the accession of linguistics to the scientific level."[4] The search for the meaning of a myth involves going beyond the familiar pattern of events; just as the succession of phonemes /t/ plus /r/ plus /i:/ is associated with a meaning "tree" impossible to derive from phonetic elements, in Oedipus' story the narration of monster slaying, parricide, and incest is but an arbitrary sequence behind which lurks the unexpected meaning: the hesitation between the biological and chthonian origin of man. The analogy is striking; nonetheless the attack on prestructuralist anthropology misfires, since the principle of arbitrariness maintains only that there is no motivated link between the conceptual side and the phonetic side of a linguistic sign; it does not deny the stability of linguistic meaning, once the semiotic system has been established. The objection to Jungian methodology fails, since not only is there nothing "un-Saussurean" about granting a set of elements a constant meaning but, on the contrary, within the Saussurean framework semantic stability constitutes a universal trait of semiotic systems.

If, in order to upgrade its scientific status, mythological analysis needs linguistic models, it still has to decide which aspect of language would provide the most appropriate term of comparison. If mythological patterns were modeled after phonemes, they would lack independent meaning, and, just as phonemes constitute and distinguish morphemes, mythological patterns would play an important role in structuring the units of higher meaningful levels. But of course mythological patterns are not meaningless in themselves. Moreover, while in linguistic systems the morphological level enjoys more visibility than does phonology—in order to grasp the meaning of an utterance we naturally tend to pass through sound without noticing it—where would one find a credible candidate for a higher mythological level, both heterogeneous and arbitrarily linked to mythological patterns? If the linguistic analogy is to be pursued, mythological patterns would better be compared to words, which possess meaning and contribute to the global meaning of the next level, the sentential level, which in turn may be used to describe states of affairs and events. Or perhaps it would be even more fruitful to assume that, in spite of superficial resemblances with word and sentence structure, myths, stories, and more generally discourse phenomena observe much more complex regularities; so their analysis needs a conceptual apparatus considerably richer than sentence linguistics can provide. By basing their inquiry strictly on phonological models, structuralists may have stopped short of exploring genuinely interesting paths for the study of myths and other discursive phenomena. Therefore, rather than accusing them of having extended scientific methods too far into the realm of the humanities, one may feel that they have failed to develop a sufficient methodological momentum and have prematurely arrested their inquiry.[5]

From anthropology, the structuralist quest for linguistic models, mediated by narrative analysis, spread into poetics, with phonologism providing a comfortable methodological solution, as can be seen in Roland Barthes's early work on narrative structures and in early literary semiotics. In literary structuralism, however, methodology was not destined to be a major concern; rather than scrutinizing the methodological adequacy of their model, most proponents of this trend preferred to theorize about general properties of literature, with the nontrivial consequence that the structuralist heritage consists more in theoretical theses than, as many believe, in a set of scientific methods. Among these theses, the most widespread have been mythocentrism, semantic fundamentalism, and the doctrine of the centrality of text, with its corollaries, an antiexpressive stand and an immanentist approach to culture. Although each was at the origin of illuminating proposals concerning myth and literature, they entailed nonetheless a limitation of research horizons.

According to mythocentrism, narrative form constitutes a privileged manifestation of literary meaning; narrative structures are set in the center of literary studies, and stylistic and rhetorical features, referential force, and social relevance are deemed to be more or less accidental. I would, moreover, distinguish between a weak, or literary, form of mythocentrism and a stronger, generalized form. Weak or literary mythocentrism may be characterized as the strategy of focusing the literary inquiry on narrative phenomena, so as to marginalize other aspects of the text and to make them appear dependent on plot. Barthes's contention that mimesis is a contingent aspect of stories, entirely subordinated to the narrative logic, provides a good example of this strategy:

> The function of narrative is not to "represent"; it is to constitute a spectacle still very enigmatic for us, but in any case not of a mimetic order. The "reality" of a sequence lies not in the "natural" succession of the actions composing it, but in the logic there exposed, risked and satisfied. (1966, pp. 123–124)

In a similar vein, literary characters have been treated as mere agents, structurally defined in relation to the units of plot.

Taking a further step in this direction, stronger or generalized mythocentrism postulates the existence of a narrative level in every meaningful event, be it a story, a nonliterary text, or even a nonlinguistic semiotic object: a painting, a musical work, a social system. It argues that textual meaning does not originate in the production of utterances and their combination into discourse; rather it is relayed on its way by narrative structures that in turn produce the meaningful discourse articulated in utterances (Greimas, 1970, p. 159). As a consequence of so powerful a hypothesis about the inner organization of semiotic systems, the proponents of strong mythocentrism relax the notion of narrative structure and allow for the identification of a narrative level in nonnarrative texts.[6] The obvious predicament of such theoretical maneuvers lies in the choice between loss of specificity and instant refutation; for, if all texts must contain narrative configurations, then either the definition of these will become general to the point of being trivial, or else the empirical existence of texts without narrative properties will disprove the hypothesis.

It was literary mythocentrism that, perhaps because of its weaker form, more extensively affected classical structuralist poetics. By overemphasizing the logic of plot, mythocentrism helped to create the impression that problems of reference, mimesis, and more generally of relations between literary texts and reality were merely aftereffects of a referential illusion, spontaneously projected by narrative syntax. This belief effectively prevented the structuralists from devoting attention to the referential properties of literary texts. Since, moreover, structuralist poetics had adopted the distinction between *story* and *discourse,* the story being most often identified with narrative structures, it was quite natural that the only alternative to plot studies were the examination of discursive techniques, an examination that, while producing remarkable accomplishments,[7] helped nevertheless to implement the moratorium on representational topics.

This moratorium was encouraged by a doctrine that I will call semantic fundamentalism and that closely relates to phonologism in mythological studies and narrative theory. During the mid- and late nineteen-fifties, when anthropological and literary structuralism came into the open, the only available framework in narratology was Vladimir Propp's study of Russian fairytales. Propp had noticed that fairytales displaying a different inventory of motifs may be described as possessing a similar sequence of abstract narrative functions. There are four sequences of events at the beginning of different tales:

(1) The king gives the hero an eagle—the eagle carries the hero to another country.

(2) Grandfather gives Suchenko a horse—the horse carries Suchenko to another country.

(3) A magician gives Ivan a boat—the boat carries Ivan to another kingdom.

(4) The queen gives Ivan a ring—strong men coming out of the ring carry Ivan to another kingdom.

These can be reduced to two abstract functions: *gift* and *departure*. The examination of a corpus of fairytales led Propp to establish a sequence of thirty-one functions shared by the members of his corpus. But, since these abstract functions were designed to capture the syntactic, combinatorial properties of the stories in question, by virtue of their very construction they fostered neglect of the specific meaning of each story.[8]

Quite early, structuralists realized that narrative and mythological semantics falls outside the scope of Proppian narratology;[9] the semantic models they proposed for myths and literary texts nonetheless share the Proppian orientation toward abstract, general schemata.

One of the most typical structuralist approaches to textual meaning is, again, Lévi-Strauss's analysis of the Oedipus myth. Inspired by the idea of the phonological oppositions that distinguish lexical units, the analysis assumes that every myth or story is underlain by a pair of achronic semantic oppositions, which constitute the semantic core of the story or myth and do not depend on the chronological unfolding of the story. Accordingly, Oedipus' myth is reduced to the linkage of two semantic oppositions: the overrating of kinship relations versus its underrating and the chthonian versus the biological origin of man. A few events of the myth are selected and distributed among these four categories: Oedipus' and Jocasta's marriage as well as Antigone's love for her brother Polynice manifest the overrating of family relations, while the killings of Laios by his son Oedipus and of Polynice by his brother Eteocles reveal the underrating of kinship links. In a less apparent way, Oedipus' victory over the Sphinx, who is a chthonian monster, and the meaning of Oedipus' name ("swollen foot") are assumed to signal respectively the negation and the affirmation of the chthonian origin of man. The global meaning of Oedipus' myth would consist in just this proportion: overrating kinship is to its underrating as affirmation of the chthonian origin of man is to its negation. Myth does not solve the tensions; rather it helps cultures to live with them, by linking oppositions to one another and relativizing them. A similiar semantic account of literary texts has been developed by structuralist semioticians who, at the deepest core of all texts and semiotic objects, postulate a four-term, semantic structure. Labeled the "semiotic square," the four-term structure is supposed to inform the meaning of the entire text through a complex generational process.[10] But neither proposal offers an explicit procedure for discovering the fundamental structure of a text, or at least for validating the proposed semantic core by confronting it with the narrative text; both inductive and deductive constraints on the analysis are disturbingly absent. The four semantic terms of the myth are obtained only through the exclusion of several events of considerable intuitive importance: the plague in Thebes, Oedipus' quest for truth, its revelation, and the hero's self-punishment. But since there is no explicit reason for the exclusion, this particular choice appears arbitrary.

More seriously, it is difficult to believe that all myths, stories, or texts can be reduced to single elementary semantic structures consisting of four terms in a proportional relationship.[11] Semiotic objects are complex constructions, overloaded with meaning; to postulate so rudimentary a sense involves a considerable loss of information; since, too, semantic fundamentalism brings no independent evidence that would confirm the existence of a core semantic structure, there are no compelling reasons to accept its oversimplifying account of the meaning of myths and stories. The absence of independent evidence is a symptom of immanentism: under the influence of early structural linguistics, in particular of Louis Hjelmslev's views, semantic fundamentalists tend to believe in the autonomy of semiotic objects to the extent that they willfully limit the inquiry to the examination of these objects, claiming that evidence about the structure of a myth should be found in the family of myths it belongs to; or that the meaning of a literary text should be discovered through the interrogation of that text only.

The belief in the autonomy of semiotic objects goes beyond the goals and practices of semantic fundamentalism; it constitutes a general feature of many recent trends in literary criticism that share a propensity to grant literary texts the central place in literary studies. The centrality of the text, as opposed to the romantic centrality of the artist, has indeed been the most widespread doctrine in literary criticism until recently. Aestheticism's and formalism's disdain for nonaesthetic values and objects, phenomenology's avoidance of history and its practice of describing isolated objects of consciousness, as well as the cult of tangible facts embraced by empiricism, have all encouraged this doctrine. In its extreme form, emphasis on single texts gives rise to the principle of "text closure," which asserts that all the elements necessary for the understanding of a text are contained therein. When practice led researchers to look for information outside the text itself, as is indispensable for the study of genres, influence, imitation, and parody, the recourse to external sources was restricted to other texts: hence the idea of intertextuality.[12]

As a consequence, the venerable notion of literary work *(oeuvre)* fell into dispute for a while. But while works are produced by craftsmen, texts can be conceived of as the result of linguistic games more or less independent of individual will and purpose: the notion of author, Barthes claimed, must give way to that of scriptor, the faceless agent through whom language deploys its textual virtualities (1968a, pp. 147–148). A strongly antiexpressive aesthetics accompanied classical structuralist poetics, discouraging reflection on those literary and artistic features that transcend purely structural properties: style, reference, representation, global meaning, expressiveness.[13]

## *Toward a Referential Theory of Fiction*

Structuralist poetics started as a rejuvenation project, confident that the right amount of linguistic ideas and methodology would infuse new life into literary studies. Some of the doctrines it gradually adopted (phonologism, mythocentrism, semantic fundamentalism, textolatry, and the antiexpressive stand) led nevertheless to a premature arrest of the theoretical advances and convinced those scholars who, in spite of their disenchantment with structuralism, were not yet prepared to abandon the ideals of rational inquiry and methodological awareness, that they had to turn elsewhere for new sources of theoretical insight. Given the perennial influence of linguistics on literary structuralism, an obvious choice was offered by transformational-generative grammar, whose theoretical endowment included a devastating critique of structuralism in linguistics.[14] Several domains directly benefited from the impact of transformational-generative linguistics upon literary studies: stylistics, plot-grammar, theoretical contributions to such notions as the generation of literary texts, deep structures, or literary competence. Situated at the confluence of formal grammar and discourse analysis, text-grammar explored formal properties of transsentential phenomena, many of which bear a direct relevance to literary texts.[15]

The attempts of transformational-generative grammarians to add a semantic component to their theory rendered the scholars involved in these loosely connected literary projects sensitive to recent analytical philosophy and formal semantics. The relevance of philosophical logic, of possible-world semantics, of speech-act theory, and of world-version epistemology could not escape researchers looking for powerful and elegant models for literary semantics. The mid- and late seventies witnessed a flurry of proposals concerning the study of narrative and literary meaning along the lines of formal semantics and philosophical logic.[16] A debate began to develop which showed that the neglected topics of literary reference, fictional worlds, and narrative content can be addressed from a new, unexpected angle. It suggested that formal semantic models and, more generally, rapprochement to philosophical results in the domain of fiction can provide for better accounts in various areas of narratology and stylistics. This line of research has not limited itself to proposing alternative answers to structuralist queries; it has also expanded its own horizon of interrogations. Questions such as literary truth, the nature of fictionality, distance and resemblance between literature and reality, neglected during the previous period, have again begun to attract the attention of theorists.

The present context in literary criticism is one in which the earlier preoccupation with the mechanics of texts is gradually being replaced by renewed interest in higher-order literary interpretation, in the multiplicity of readings, in hermeneutics and ideology. The right to be subjective is widely recognized; serious doubts are being raised about the possibility of scientific attitudes in the literary field; the reader's position in the literary exchange is being considerably enhanced; last but not least, by stressing the relevance of literature for issues of immediate human concern, the advent of feminist criticism has restored the respectability of thematic criticism. In this new configuration, literary theory has to confront an entire range of issues that were beyond the scope of classical structuralism. It must reexamine conventionalist assumptions and tackle again the problem of the representation of reality in fiction. The moratorium on referential issues has by now become obsolete. Freed from the constraints of the textualist approach, theory of fiction can respond again to the world-creating powers of imagination and account for the properties of fictional existence and worlds, their complexity, incompleteness, remoteness, and integration within the general economy of culture.

These topics constitute the subject matter of this book. Some of its themes echo the philosophical discussion about fiction, while others derive from longstanding literary concerns. I have attempted to blend components in the hope that the result will enhance the interest of literary scholars in recent philosophical work on fiction.[17]

# 2 〰 Fictional Beings

THE second chapter of *The Pickwick Papers* opens with these sentences:

> That punctual servant of all work, the sun, had just risen and begun
> to strike a light on the morning of the thirteenth of May, one thousand
> eight hundred and twenty-seven, when Mr. Samuel Pickwick burst
> like another sun from his slumbers, threw open his chamber window,
> and looked out upon the world beneath. Goswell Street was at his
> feet, Goswell Street extended on his left; and the opposite side of
> Goswell Street was over the way.

The reader of this passage experiences two contradictory intuitions:
on the one hand he knows well that unlike the sun, whose actual
existence is beyond doubt, Mr. Pickwick and most of the human
beings and states of affairs described in the novel do not and never
did exist outside its pages. On the other hand, once Mr. Pickwick's
fictionality is acknowledged, happenings inside the novel are vividly
felt as possessing some sort of reality of their own, and the reader
can fully sympathize with the adventures and reflections of the characters.

To account for this intuitive predicament, philosophers of fiction
have proposed several answers that reflect various epistemological
attitudes toward the relations between reality and fiction. Some theoreticians promote a segregationist view of these relations, characterizing the content of fictional texts as pure imagination without truth
value; their opponents adopt a tolerant, integrationist outlook, claiming that no genuine ontological difference can be found between fictional and nonfictional descriptions of the actual world. Each tendency
is well represented in philosophical discussions and, certainly, be-

tween them there is room for several intermediate or mixed positions. While old-fashioned segregationists reject fictional discourse on ontological grounds and assume that since Mr. Pickwick does not exist, the novel is false or spurious, a new segregationist stand makes use of speech-act theory and recommends a separation based on differences between genres of discourse, claiming that the quoted passage would instantiate a specific way of speaking or writing, as opposed to factual reporting. The integrationists, in turn, in particular those belonging to the conventionalist persuasion, may be motivated by unbounded confidence in the ontological weight of fictional discourse and assume that Mr. Pickwick enjoys an existence barely less substantial than the sun or England in 1827. Otherwise they take a diffident view of textual accounts and undercut the distinction between fiction and other species of discourse, by considering all texts as equally governed by arbitrary conventions; so a treatise on the history of early nineteenth-century England is not to be trusted any more than Dickens' *Pickwick Papers,* since in its own way each text simply describes a version of the world.

Be they of a segregationist, integrationist, or any of the intermediary persuasions, philosophers often examine fiction only indirectly, in passing, and in relation to other theoretical queries; in many cases their positions regarding fiction derive from philosophical concerns that are quite extraneous to literary interests. During the following discussion, then, it may be useful to keep in mind a threefold conceptual distinction in order to understand the main thrust of various philosophical arguments. One should differentiate between *metaphysical* questions about fictional beings and truth; *demarcational* questions regarding the possibility of establishing sharp boundaries between fiction and nonfiction, both in theory and in practical criticism; and *institutional* questions related to the place and importance of fiction as a cultural institution. Philosophers of various orientations do not uniformly answer these three sets of questions: segregationist stands on the demarcational problem can be associated with various ontological choices. Moreover, neither ontology nor the demarcational stand necessarily determines a philosopher's attitude toward fiction as an institution. Traditionally, severe segregationism went together with a certain amount of disregard for the spurious work of the imagination, but this need not be the case for many modern segregationists, who may reject fictional entities and look for demarcation while still believing that fiction plays an important role in our lives.

## Classical Segregationism

The classical segregationist view reflects the worries of early analytical philosophy regarding the nature of language and its links to the world. Built up during a period when the philosophy of logic and science estimated that its most urgent tasks included securing sound foundations and protection against neo-Hegelian idealism, this view displayed a pronounced bias in favor of economy in ontology and a normative attitude in logic. According to classical segregationists, there is no universe of discourse outside the real world. Existence, which is not a predicate, can be ascribed only to objects of the actual world. Since human linguistic practices offer so many examples of reference to imaginary objects, from myths to novels and from erroneous scientific hypotheses to verbose philosophical constructions, there must be something wrong with our language that allows the endless proliferation of *entia rationis*. Examination of nonreferring expressions shows that, mischevously disguised as definite descriptions, they cannot be linguistically distinguished from fully referring expressions, as the following examples show:

(1) The present president of France is wise.

(2) The present king of France is wise.

(3) Mr. Pickwick is wise.

In spite of their linguistic similarity, the first sentence, in 1986 at least, contains a reference to an actual being, while the second and the third do not. Bertrand Russell exposed the logical structure of the three sentences by paraphrasing them as follows.

(4) There exists one and only one entity such that the entity is the present president of France and whatever is the present president of France is wise.

(5) There exists one and only one entity such that the entity is the present king of France and whatever is the present king of France is wise.

(6) There exists one and only one entity such that the entity is Mr. Pickwick and whatever is Mr. Pickwick is wise.

Each of these sentences is treated as a conjunction that first asserts that there exists one and only one entity having the property of being the president of France, or the king of that country, or Mr. Pickwick;

and second, that the entity in question is wise. To establish the truth of the first half of each sentence, we must in each case ascertain that there indeed is one and only one entity displaying one of the above-mentioned properties: we must, in other words, scan the universe in search of the entity. If performed on the 1986 slice of the universe, the result of the search will be a gentleman named François Mitterrand for sentence (4) and no entity for the last two sentences. Extending the search to the four-dimensional space-time continuum, we will in addition find a series of creatures enjoying the property of being the "present king of France." Yet, no matter how carefully we look, no entity displaying the property of being Mr. Pickwick will ever be found: the sentence turns out to be false before we even may consider its second part. As conjunctions that have a false first half, statements about fictional entities are false, Russell claimed, independently of their predicative content, simply by virtue of their logical structure.[1]

Russell's answer to the metaphysical question consists in denying nonexistent individuals any ontological status, and in proving that statements about such individuals are false on logical grounds. Without specifically addressing the demarcational question, his stand results in the exclusion of statements about fictional entities from the realm of true discourse, with the implied consequence that the semantics of fictionality is of little philosophical interest. His stand does not entail a negative answer to the institutional question since, like most educated people, Russell does not deny fiction, as an institution, a certain importance in our lives; yet his philosophy provides little encouragement for research on the semantics of fiction. And it is not by chance that literary theorists attempting to come to grips with Russellian segregationism have had to devise various strategies for explaining fictional statements in noncognitive terms; Richards' "emotive" theory of literature comes to mind.[2]

A more nuanced segregationist approach takes into consideration the speech situation; set in its context of use, a sentence like "The present king of France is wise" can be true if uttered by a subject of Henry IV, false if pronounced by a contemporary of Charles IX, and spurious if asserted in contemporary republican France. This approach, which originates in P. F. Strawson's criticism of Russellian analysis,[3] allows for truth-value gaps and spurious statements, and therefore involuntarily leads to an even more severe segregation between fictional and nonfictional statements; for, while under Russell's treatment fiction is attributed the truth value false and therefore conserves a minimal logical respectability, in Strawson's account fictional statements fall into the category of permanently spurious sentences. According to this analysis, at least during monarchic periods "The present king of France is wise" achieves the logical feat of possessing a truth-value; by contrast, "Mr. Pickwick is wise" never overcomes its built-in spuriousness.

Although Strawson's papers do not primarily focus on fictional entities, their consequences for the theory of fiction are not difficult to draw; they are corroborated in an early paper by Gilbert Ryle,[4] which expresses a similar position in greater detail and more specifically directed at imaginary objects. Ryle noticed that propositions about Mr. Pickwick, at least those found in *The Pickwick Papers*, contain a designating term and a series of predicates. But some expressions and sentences simply look like designations when they are not and should not be taken as such. "When Dickens says 'Mr. Pickwick wore knee-breeches,' the proper name seems to designate someone; but if no one was called 'Mr. Pickwick,' then the proposition can't be true or false of the man called Mr. Pickwick. For there was no one so called. And then the proposition is not really about someone" (p. 26). Since they contain pseudo-designations, fictional statements are not true or false in the ordinary, nonmetaphorical sense. And since fictional names have no denotata and fictional statements containing them lack truth-value, "nothing is left as a metaphysical residue to be housed in an ontological no-man's-land" (p. 35).

The segregationist attitude can be better understood if it is remembered that Russell's theory of descriptions has been designed for specific philosophical needs, in a context in which a strong control over language was required. To maintain such control seems indispensable for areas and periods in which a sense of responsibility must be preserved, such as, according to a widespread view, was the case at the turn of the century in the philosophy of mathematics, logic, and the exact sciences. But the criteria and restrictions applicable in these situations do not necessarily fit all fields of inquiry; in particular, the requirements of aesthetics and poetics may well be less stringent than those of the philosophy of mathematics and science, and in studying fictional statements tolerance may be the most appropriate attitude. Since every reader trivially accepts that Mr. Pickwick does not designate an inhabitant of the actual world, to build up defenses against fictional entities may be a waste of energy, at least as long as the discussion focuses on aesthetic and poetic topics. And while in dealing with scientific concepts one may feel justified in eliminating nonexistent entities, the poetics of fiction needs a technique for *introducing* such entities. The purpose of the poetics of fiction cannot consist of the purification of language and ontology: on the contrary, poetics must account for unregimented linguistic practices and construct appropriate descriptive models to help us understand what happens when we use fictional statements. Ryle's satisfaction that his account of imaginary beings leaves nothing as "a metaphysical residue to be housed in an ontological no-man's-land" is little warranted. For, depending on their priorities and concerns, researchers of fiction can adopt two different courses. On the one hand, they may choose an external approach that would relate fiction to a more general theory of being and truth; in this case, since the ontology of the nonfictional world would prevail, fictional names would lack denotata, fictional statements would be false or spurious, and metaphysical segregationism would be vindicated. On the other hand, an internal approach is conceivable, which would not so much aim at comparing fictional entities and statements with their nonfictional counterparts (for, obviously, a comparison of this sort would have to admit the vacuity of fictional names and the falsity or spuriousness of statements about them) as at constructing a model that represents the *users'* understanding of fiction once they step inside it and more or less lose touch with the nonfictional realm. And, clearly, an internal approach should not avoid exploring Ryle's no-man's-land and providing adequate housing for the entities wandering in it.

When addressing the demarcational problem independently of purely metaphysical concerns, it must be noted that, although an external approach would perhaps be justified in drawing a sharp *theoretical* distinction between fictional and nonfictional statements, well-defined borders between these two kinds of statements are counterintuitive when dealing with specific fictional texts from an internal point of view. During the reading of *The Pickwick Papers* does Mr. Pickwick appear less real than the sun over Goswell Street? In *War and Peace* is Natasha less actual than Napoleon? Fictional texts enjoy a certain discursive unity; for their readers, the worlds they describe are not necessarily fractured along a fictive/actual line.

Equally difficult, especially within the economy of an internal approach, is the logical atomists' habit of considering fictional texts as collections of sentences, each individually responsible for its logical status and truth-value. In a typical passage Ryle asks:

> What or whom are the propositions about which readers propound when they say 'Mr. Pickwick did not visit Oxford'? Clearly, their propositions are about the book, or the propositions printed on the pages of the book. They are saying, in a shorthand way, 'None of the sentences in the book says or implies that Mr. Pickwick visited Oxford.' This is shown by the fact that in case of a dispute settlement will be looked for and reached by simple reading of the text. (p. 28)

In a move that recalls the structuralist text-closure principle, the book is identified with the sentences printed on its pages. But this goes against the elementary intuitions of most writers and readers, who are less inclined to ask questions about Mr. Pickwick visiting Oxford than about, say, Mr. Pickwick being obnoxious or generous or absent-minded or stubborn, or about Sam Weller's father being a delightful or an insufferable misogynist. To these questions, which are among the simplest that could be raised by a reader or critic, one cannot answer by simply inspecting the propositions printed on the pages of the book. An inference system is needed that would relate passages of the book to an extratextual cultural and factual framework. More complex interpretations of literary texts are of course even less easily linked to the set of printed propositions.

Literary texts, like most informal collections of sentences, such as conversations, newspaper articles, eyewitness testimony, history books, biographies of famous people, myths, and literary criticism, display a property that may puzzle logicians but that doubtless appears natural to anyone else: their truth as a whole is not recursively definable starting from the truth of the individual sentences that constitute them. Global truth is not simply derived from the local truth-value of the sentences present in the text. An excellent biography of Nelson can be called true overall, even if we find a few factual errors in it; similarly, eyewitness testimony in a complex murder case is generally taken as true, despite a few incorrect details. Moreover, a text can possess more than one level of meaning. A myth or an allegorical text consisting mostly or even only of false sentences can nevertheless be felt as allegorically true as a whole. It is therefore useless to set up procedures for assessing the truth or falsity of isolated fictional sentences, since their micro-truth value may well have no impact on the macro-truth value of large segments of the text or on the text as a totality.

## The Speech-Act Theory of Fiction

The notion of context of use, as introduced by Strawson, gives classical segregationism a supplement of flexibility; subsequent developments in speech-act theory provided for a systematic account of pragmatic factors in linguistic exchange, and offered segregationism a fresh theoretical framework for separating fictional discourse from factual statements.

The success of speech-act theory has encouraged contacts between analytical philosophy and literary criticism; it has stimulated reflection on the definition of literature and literary genres, contributed extensively to analyses of poetry and drama, and served as a basis for a semantic approach to fiction.[5] One of the earliest attempts to apply speech-act notions to literary theory is Richard Ohmann's search for a nontrivial definition of literature (1971, 1972). Ohmann's argument displays an interesting structure, often found in the application of formal models to literary phenomena. This kind of argument, which I would call the "model breakdown" approach, consists of three operations: it is first claimed that literature is a subclass of a more general field; second, a model of this field is expounded; third, it is shown that literary phenomena cannot be satisfactorily encompassed within the range of distinctions offered by the model. The breakdown of the model is assumed to tell us something significant about literature. In Ohmann's argument, since literature is a verbal endeavor, J. L. Austin's model of speech acts should be relevant to literary discourse as well. However, when one considers literature, Austin's categories significantly fail to apply. Consequently, "a literary work is a discourse whose sentences lack the illocutionary forces that would normally attach to them. Its illocutionary force is mimetic" (p. 14). In the same vein, Barbara Herrnstein Smith argues that fiction does not just fill another slot in the typology of speech acts, but it incorporates the full range of speech acts, with a change in the key signature: fictional texts consist of represented speech acts (1978, pp. 14–40).

The model-breakdown argument, as well as the idea that fiction instantiates a kind of speech act that does not fit into the normal range, play an important role in the theory of fictional discourse propounded by John Searle and, independently, by Gottfried Gabriel. The discussion bears upon the metaphysical problem insofar as the two philosophers examine whether the author who writes the sentences of a fictional text is making assertions that might be true or false, but the main thrust of Searle's and Gabriel's account relates to the problem of demarcation, since they attempt to establish a sharp theoretical distinction between fictional and nonfictional discourse. These two writers start from the assumption that fictional discourse is a type of utterance and that reference takes place only in relation to correct utterances. Limiting their discussion to assertive utterances, the two authors propose a set of rules that govern the correctness of these utterances:

(1) The essential rule: the speaker commits himself to the truth of his assertion. While Searle does not define commitment, Gabriel requires that the speaker must accept the consequences of his utterance. We shall see, however, that this is an exorbitantly severe rule.

(2) The preparatory rule: the speaker must be capable of defending the truth of the assertion. Gabriel calls this condition "the rule of argumentation."

(3) The proposition expressed by the assertion must not be obviously true to the participants in the communicative situation; this is a rule of politeness, closely ressembling Grice's maxims of quantity.

(4) The sincerity rule: according to Searle, the speaker must commit himself to a belief in the truth of the expressed proposition. Presumably, the difference between (1) and (4) is the logical commitment to the truth of an assertion and the moral commitment to believing its content.

The two writers then argue that in fictional discourse these rules are not respected. There is little reason to believe that Dickens felt committed to the truth of most sentences contained in *The Pickwick Papers* or sincerely believed them; an author is rarely able to defend the truth of his assertions or to accept the consequences of his fictional utterances. In fact, Searle claims, the author of a novel only *pretends* to make assertions without actually making them. Even if these pretensions are of a benign kind, since they do not attempt to deceive, fictional assertions fall outside the class of assertion-making utterances. Nonetheless, serious statements can be conveyed by pretended speech acts, not unlike the way in which indirect speech acts imply genuine ones (Searle, 1975a). A sentence like "Can you pass the salt?" also means "Please pass the salt." Similarly, the wisdom about marriage derived from *Anna Karenina* is indirectly conveyed by the pretended statements of the novel.

One of the interesting aspects of the Searle–Gabriel account consists in shifting the emphasis of the discussion about fiction onto its pragmatic features. While in a Russellian framework segregation rests on ontological and logical grounds, the speech-act theory derives fictionality from the linguistic attitude of the speaker; and since virtually any sentence or sequence thereof can be uttered as mere pretense, Searle's and Gabriel's arguments appear to play down the existence of intrinsically fictional discourse. Due to various historical reasons, many texts are read fictionally, thus providing an indirect confirmation of their approach. (However, Walton rightly argued that their insistence on the speaker's role in defining fiction is difficult to accept, since when we read a serious text as fiction, we neglect the author's intention.) In addition, their use of pretense has the advantage of calling attention to the playful component of fictional discourse; it also insists that fiction is an activity rather than a mere list of peculiar sentences. Yet the arguments of discursive segregationists are not free of difficulties: one might cast doubt on the correctness of the rules of assertion, on the notion of speaker as originator of fictional discourse, and on the very notion of pretense in relation to fiction.

Designed as idealizations that account for normal or serious uses of language, the rules for assertion are intended to discriminate against what Austin called "parasitical" or "etiolated" uses. In order to follow the sincerity rule scrupulously, a speaker has to be transparent to himself with respect to his beliefs; but since his linguistic competence enables a speaker to utter an astronomically large number of assertions, the sincere speaker must possess a set of propositions he believes in, and a machinery able to select quickly for each of the assertive utterances the corresponding sentence belonging to the set believed to be true. When the speaker utters a sentence, the machine is automatically triggered: if the result of its scanning the set of sentences believed to be true is successful, the speaker may be said to have been sincere; if the machine fails to find the corresponding sentence, the speaker has been insincere.

But do real speakers possess anything like a set of propositions they believe to be true, possibly accompanied by an inference procedure? On the contrary, the picture we get from actual situations indicates that we more or less believe a limited number of propositions, without knowing whether we believe their consequences or not, and for a large number of propositions we simply do not know, in any serious sense of the word, whether we believe them to be true or not. In many cases we assert sentences we think we believe in, when in fact we only adhere to these sentences for reasons other than belief; for instance, we may only admire the person whom we heard assert these sentences. I can utter with conviction sentences like:

(5)  The best vacation spot in Germany is Baden-Baden.

(6)  Most of Shakespeare's plays were written by his wife.

without ever having seriously examined their content. These may be my friend Gloss's professed opinions, and I feel I have the right to see them as my own, perhaps as a way of showing my attachment to Gloss.

When setting an idealized condition requiring that the speaker commit himself to the truth of his assertion, do we ask the speaker to believe deeply in its truth, or are we prepared to allow for a perfunctory assent of the speaker to his own sayings? Is the belief supposed to last for a long time, or are we satisfied with a belief equal in duration to the utterance believed to be true? Should the belief be simultaneous with the utterance, or may it precede or follow the assertion?

These are not spurious questions induced by the mere difference between idealization and performance. Philosophers have widely discussed the assuredness of our knowledge and beliefs, allowing for more elaborate criteria than mere commitment to belief in the truth of a sentence. H. H. Price distinguished among *opinion, conviction,* and *absolute conviction.* In answer to Norman Malcolm's assumption that being confident about one's knowledge is an essential feature of knowledge, A. D. Woozley and Alan White argued against the psychologizing of knowledge and in favor of dissociating the feeling of certitude from knowledge. Such a dissociation applies to belief as well: Price proposes the illuminating distinction between *belief proper,* characterized as assent upon evidence, and mere *acceptance* or *taking for granted,* which he describes as an "unreasoned absence of dissent."[6] Do we require our speakers properly to believe their sentences to be true? If their life depended on rejecting them, would we allow them to retract? What if a speaker, like many of Thomas Mann's characters, simply plays with the idea that he believes his sentence to be true, and when confronted with the pressing question "Do you really believe this?" answers "I don't know. My friends say that," or "I saw it in the newspaper," or "They said it on TV."

Our sincerity shows less commitment to an assertion than loyalty to our friends, to our sources, to the social group that professes it. Hilary Putnam has pointed out that a given community collectively masters its language and the relation between it and reality (1965, 1973). As an individual, a member of the community may not fully master the use of terms like *elm, gnosis,* or *werewolf,* in the sense that he or she may not be in the possession of the means for determining whether an object is an elm, a gnosis, or a werewolf. According to Putnam, one can employ such terms, nevertheless, by virtue of the social division of linguistic labor. An ignoramus may refer to *elms, gnosis,* and *werewolves* on the assumption that the community hosts specialists in elms, gnosis, and werewolves who can provide all the information necessary should the need arise for a closer scrutiny of statements about these entities. But this means that in order to make assertions, one has less need of commitment to the truth of particular statements than *epistemological adherence* to the linguistic practice of a given community.

What has been said about sincerity applies even more to the preparatory and the essential rules. How can we ask our unreliable speakers to defend the truth of their utterances or to accept their consequences? Speakers who are sincere by participation should not be expected to defend the truth of most of their utterances other than by reference to the community or to accept readily the consequences of what they say. We do not individually possess qualities such as sincerity, ability to argue about assertions, and readiness to accept their consequences, except for a very limited range of sentences. Most often we behave as if our personal linguistic duties had somehow been waived; we do not always need to perform these duties scrupulously, since at every failure to do so the community is there to back us up.

But, if so, the very notion of the speaker as the unique originator and master of his own utterances becomes difficult to maintain. The contemporary linguistic notion of an ideal speaker in possession of an elaborate linguistic competence, knowing his syntax, the meanings of words, the speech-act rules controlling his beliefs and expectations, is a modern offshoot of the Cartesian subject, that motionless master of an inner space entirely under his control. In recent years criticism coming from various quarters, including Jacques Lacan's psychology, Jacques Derrida's attack against the notion of presence-to-oneself, and the deconstructionist rejection of meaning control, has severely undermined this conception. Interestingly, Putnam's approach, while originating in analytical philosophy and its preoccupation with a well-constrained, transparent language, leads to similar conclusions: when seen as a member of a linguistic community that largely covers for his utterances, the individual speaker appears to be much less distinctively in charge of his assertions than the Cartesian tradition maintains.[7]

In any case, there are few areas where the Cartesian notion of a subject-speaker is less appropriate than literary utterances. Speech-act theorists neglect the persistent testimony of storytellers, bards, poets, and writers who so often mention a *vicarious speech experience* as a central aspect of poetic acts. The muse may have become a worn-out symbol, more often ridiculed than actually used: reference to the muse nonetheless is far from spurious. Like the prophet's reliance on his god, the poet's reference to the muse, to inspiration, to the dictation of the subconscious, is a way of mentioning this particular type of speech, in which the speaker is spoken through by a voice that is not exactly his own.

Plato, in *Ion,* describes such an experience. But perhaps it is not at all necessary to have recourse to the poetics of enthusiasm in this context. To show that the Cartesian image of a well-individualized speaker in full control of his voice does not fit the production of literary fiction, it may be enough to think of the complexity and elusiveness of the originating voice in literary discourse.[8] The writer as an individual, the authorial voice, the narrator, reliable or not, the voices of the characters, distinct from one another or more or less mixed together, undercut any attempt to comment on fiction as if it had one well-individuated originator.

Turning now to the notion of pretense, I want to argue that the distinction between pretended and genuine acts often becomes blurred in relation to fiction. Consider a performance by a mime who pretends to be a priest and blesses the audience. Is the blessing genuine? Certainly not, so long as the act remains within the limits of normality and both the actor and the audience correctly interpret its setting. But assume that the impersonation takes place in a kingdom where, against the wishes of the people, religion has been outlawed by a cruel tyrant. Churches have been closed, priests imprisoned, and true believers martyred. Further, a campaign against the old faith has been launched, which requires every artistic event to include some anti-religious feature. Our mime has accordingly been instructed to include a parody of priestly gestures in his repertoire. But like most of the inhabitants, the mime is a deeply religious man. Unable to avoid performing the blasphemous act, he decides subtly to transform it into an unobstrusive remembrance of the Mass. The audience has been deprived of any religious ceremony for so long that even an imitation of the precious forbidden gestures can be electrifying. Besides, the image of a priest is so venerable in this society without priests that the spectators instinctively neglect the parodic side of the antireligious act. So, in the midst of the performance, the mime turns toward the public and, letting a saintly expression invade his face, slowly and solemnly blesses the crowd. A stream of grace passes through the hall. No one present doubts the genuineness of the blessing. Neither do the few censors who supervise the performance; indeed, the next day the mime is arrested and executed.[9]

Was the blessing a true one? Or was it but the delusion of a deprived crowd bewitched by a skillful clown? The right conditions for the performance of the sacramental gestures were obviously not met; nevertheless the community had the right to waive these conventions spontaneously and to accept the exceptional performance, letting pretense become as effective as the genuine act.

Or think of a young man who coldly decides to seduce the wife of a friend by pretending that he is madly in love with her. Suppose that he first meets with resistance, which only increases his desire to succeed, making him more insistent in his courtship and more vigorously feign the symptoms of star-crossed love. Once his simulation reaches a certain level of intensity, however, he may well be caught in his own trap: the sentence "I love you," which he so often uttered as a pretense, may become true, and the role he played may now represent his genuine feelings.[10]

In a less dramatic instance, consider a reader of *The Pickwick Papers* who, after enjoying the passage quoted above, arrives at Mr. Pickwick's reflections upon contemplating Goswell Street:

> Such are the narrow views of those philosophers who, content with examining the things that lie before them, look not to the truths which are hidden beyond. As well might I be content to gaze on Goswell Street forever, without one effort to penetrate to the hidden countries which on every side surround it.

Suppose that our reader, being somewhat out of touch with wisdom literature, finds Mr. Pickwick's thoughts genuinely uplifting and under their influence changes his way of looking at things: would not his newly won wisdom be genuine? More generally, how can we decide which of the cultural and symbolic messages transmitted by fiction are genuine and which are pretended? Well aware of the difficulty,

Searle distinguishes between fictional statements and genuine assertions inserted by writers in stories:

> To take a famous example, Tolstoy begins *Anna Karenina* with the
> sentence "Happy families are all happy in the same way, unhappy
> families unhappy in their separate, various ways". That, I take it, is
> not a fictional, but a serious utterance. It is a genuine assertion. (pp.
> 331–332)

Unfortunately, however, authors do not always straightforwardly
express their wisdom: important gnomic passages often are put in
the mouth of a character (*le raisonneur* in French classical comedy);
on other occasions characters display their own brand of wisdom,
which from the author's point of view may appear quite fictional but
which can nevertheless appeal to readers and genuinely contribute to
their enlightenment. Mr. Pickwick's reflections radiate this kind of
fictional sagacity, indicative of a technique that later and in a different
context will be developed by Thomas Mann and Robert Musil. The
inexhaustible gnomic energy of Settembrini and Naphta in *The Magic
Mountain* or of Arnheim in *The Man Without Qualities* belongs to the
same family of effects as Mr. Pickwick's dignified thoughts. The
digressions of Settembrini, Naphta, Arnheim, or Pickwick certainly
are invented speech acts and lack "seriousness" in Searle's sense; but
perhaps invention should not be identified here with mere pretense:
like the mime's gesture, the wisdom of fictional characters can on
occasion become an authentic source of inspiration for the reader.

Thus fiction does not make its relevance felt only through "serious"
statements inserted on purpose by the writer. Rather, the mixture of
pretended and genuine statements bears a striking resemblance to
Quine's notion of theory, wherein "reference is nonsense except relative to a coordinate system" and individual elements of the theory
cannot be independently related to corresponding parts of the universe
(1969, p. 48). Like theories, fictional texts refer as systems, and just
as in physics it is often impossible to set apart "genuinely" referential
elements from the mathematical apparatus, in fiction one does not
always need to keep track of pretended and genuine statements, since
global relevance is apparent in spite of such distinctions.

## On Seriousness and Marginality

The rules of assertion, the notion of a speaker in full control of his
utterances, as well as the distinction between serious and pretended

utterances, are all based on a set of specific assumptions about our collective behavior. These rules and distinctions presuppose that collective behavior in general and communication in particular are of two well-defined types: normal or serious, opposed to marginal or nonserious; that normal or serious behavior is governed by a finite set of constitutive rules that function like social conventions and are fully known by the members of the community; that marginal or nonserious behavior involves a suspension of the serious conventions and their replacement by specific conventions of "parasitic" speech, equally well mastered by the participants. Incidentally, it is worth noticing that these assumptions are closely related to the model-breakdown argument, which functions precisely by virtue of the sharp distinction between normality and deviance. More generally, they are at the very heart of the segregationist attitude and point toward its close links with what deconstructionist critics label the "logocentric attitude," that is, the discriminatory search for normative ideality as opposed to accidents and deviations, an attitude that in Derrida's view has characterized Western metaphysics since its beginnings. Yet one does not have to emulate Derrida's followers in their radical condemnation of logocentric practices in order to notice that, advantageous as it may be in accounting for certain normative phenomena, segregationism, discursive or otherwise, tends to marginalize phenomena that do not fit its framework. By taking for granted the existence and stability of linguistic conventions, speech-act theory neglects the dynamism of their establishment and their inherent fluidity.

My arguments against the rules for assertion, the role of the speaker, and the unredeemability of pretense are meant to point toward this neglected fluidity. In contrast with segregationism, one can start theorizing from the assumption that social behavior contains an adventurous, creative side and a tendency to ossify successful novelties into the conventions of normality. Under such a view, normal and marginal behavior belong to a continuum and share a considerable number of traits; the rules in force in some society at some point in its history are by no means the only possible or definitive choice; members of the community do not master these rules entirely. Such an "integrationist" approach will lead us to consider marginal behavior as a manifestation of the creative side of social behavior, and its marginality as relative to the undue canonization of transitory normality. This would help to explain why members of the community often feel that various conventions for parasitic discourse are more general and more relevant than the conventions of normal discourse, why the mime's blessing may effectively have brought salvation to the spectators, why the young man ended up experiencing the pretended feelings, and why so many of us acquire bits of wisdom from reading *The Pickwick Papers.*

A further point worth mentioning is that, concerning the metaphysical problem, discursive segregationism does not radically differ from its ontological counterpart. Since in Searle's view normal referential practices are governed by the axiom of existence ("only what exists can be referred to"), failure of the referent to stand somewhere in the spatial-temporal continuum reflects on the very soundness of the utterance. A sentence without an actual referent will be considered defective or abnormal, and an activity that consists mainly of uttering referentially defective sentences will be regarded with suspicion and dismay. Says Searle: "It is after all an odd, peculiar and amazing fact about human language that it allows the possibility of fiction at all" (p. 325). It fortunately turns out that defectiveness of fictional discourse is not morally evil; the author of fiction does not intend to deceive, he is just indulging in what must be considered as a marginal, aberrant activity, understandable only insofar as governed by a secondary set of conventions that counteract the established rules of normality.

But when considered from an integrationist point of view, fiction ceases to be an anomaly, marginally accepted by a straightforward but tolerant speech community. Seen from this vantage point, referential behavior includes a creative, risk-taking aspect, as well as a tendency to settle down into conventional patterns. Normal and marginal referential practices belong to the same continuum and display many identical characteristics. On the farfetched assumption that there exists a community where the axiom of existence is in force, where in other words only what exists can be referred to, the axiom would represent nothing more than the normative ossification of certain referential practices. "Marginal" referential practices such as myth or fiction manifest the innovative side of referential processes and are perceived as marginal only in contrast to some culturally determined ossification into normality.

## Meinongian Theories

By transferring the puzzle of fictional beings from ontology to the domain of discourse, the speech-act theory of fiction remains compatible with Russellian orthodoxy and can dispense with nonexistent beings in its ontology. Recent years have witnessed a growing dissatisfaction with Russellian systems, a dissatisfaction that led to a search for alternative, richer ontologies. Alexis Meinong's theory of objects, one of the chief targets of Russell's attacks, has attracted renewed interest.[11] A partisan of ontological tolerance, Meinong assumed that since every actual object consists of a list of properties, one can extend the definition of objects by stipulating that to every list of properties there corresponds an object, be it existent or not. To the set of properties (goldenness, mountainhood) corresponds the object *golden mountain,* which lacks existence but which under Meinong's definition qualifies nonetheless as an object. Some sets of properties are such that objects correlated with them are impossible: a collection of features containing both squareness and roundness would correspond to the impossible square circle. But the impossibility of its actually existing does not prevent the square circle from being an object in the Meinongian theory. The list of properties related to an object still must obey certain constraints. Following Meinong's lead, Terence Parsons distinguishes between *nuclear* predicates, such as "goldenness," "mountainhood," "humanity," "detectivehood," and so on, and *extranuclear* predicates, which include ontological properties ("exists," "is mythical"), modal properties ("is possible," "is impossible"), intentional properties ("is thought about by Meinong," "is worshiped by the Greeks"), and technical properties ("is complete"). Limiting Meinongian objects to collections of nuclear properties, Parsons reserves extranuclear features for describing various arrangements of the worlds in which the Meinongian objects are included. Thus, about the golden mountain, an object possessing the nuclear properties of "goldenness" and "mountainhood," one can assert various extranuclear predicates: "does not exist," "is fictional," "is possible," "is thought about by Meinong."

In Parsons' account, fictional objects possess all nuclear properties we naively attribute to them, but they enjoy these properties only *in* the novel or text to which they belong, membership in a text being an extranuclear property. Instead of refusing creatures of fiction the ontological privilege of being an object, this theory provides them with a double status: the nuclear properties describe the properties of fictional objects within fiction, while the nonnuclear ones safely keep them out of the real world. Mr. Pickwick is nuclearly an Englishman, a bachelor, an observer of the human condition, and extranuclearly a character in Dickens' novel.

The real world, however, cannot be kept out of fictional texts:

theories of fiction often stumble up against what John Woods calls "mixed sentences" that combine real and fictional elements, either by allowing fictional beings to wander in the actual world, as in: "Freud psychoanalyzed Gradiva." Or, more often, by granting real entities the right to inhabit fiction: "in another hour, Mr. Pickwick, with his portmanteau in his hand, his telescope in his great-coat pocket, and his notebook in his waistcoat, ready for the reception of any discoveries worthy of being noted down, had arrived at the coach-stand in St. Martin's-le-Grand."

In order to confine fictional objects to their texts, Parsons distinguishes between characters or objects native to a story, immigrant objects, and surrogate objects. The natives can be extranuclearly described as invented or created by the author of the text, the way Mr. Pickwick was created by Dickens. Immigrants to the text come from elsewhere, either from the real world (St. Martin's-le-Grand and London) or from other texts (Quixote in Avellaneda's plagiarized continuation of Cervantes' novel, Iphigenia in Racine's tragedy, Doctor Faustus in various texts about him). Surrogate objects are fictional counterparts of real objects in those fictional texts that substantially modify their description: it may thus be argued that Balzac's novels describe a Paris that in a sense is different from the actual city. Of course, taking Paris in *La Fille aux yeux d'or* as a surrogate object is mutually exclusive with considering it an immigrant object. The decision is determined by our views on mimesis and realism as well as by our knowledge about extratextual entities. If we accept at their face value Balzac's claims to faithful representation of Paris, the city will simply have immigrated to his novel. In *La Femme de trente ans* Napoleon makes only a brief appearance; seen from a distance during a military parade, he visits the novel as a reflection of his real character: he is an immigrant. But is Richelieu in Dumas' *The Three Musketeers* playing his own role? How can we be sure? Does it not seem more probable that Dumas created a surrogate of the Cardinal? The difference between surrogtes and immigrants could be one of truth-to-life: while immigrants who settle in novels bring along their genuine personalities, surrogates are only well-designed dummies, more or less like the originals but irremediably interpreted and transformed by the writer. Segregationism creeps in again, in the least predictable place. Is Antony in Shakespeare's play an immigrant or a surrogate? Most critics would undoubtedly answer that he is a surrogate, since Shakespeare's poetic vision goes beyond the historical character, adding and subtracting features. But how would we then evaluate Antony in Plutarch's biography, obviously very close to Shakespeare's character and also, very likely, the product of Plutarch's moralistic and anti-Roman vision? Since the Meinongian project is an unifying one, would it not be better to play down the difficult distinction between immigrants and surrogates, especially since other features of the theory have an antisegregationist ring? According to Parsons, for example, we understand fictional texts by extrapolating the meaning of the sentences being read and constructing an integrated account, which is gradually modified and expanded during the reading, leading to a final result, the maximal account. We infer the maximal account from the reading of texts by virtue of "some principle of total evidence . . . based on what they say, together with what we know about their situation and about the world" (Parsons, 1980, pp. 179–180).

A theory of fictional entities constructed along these lines presents the considerable advantage of not eliminating them from the realm of beings. By making ontological commitments to imaginary beings, Meinongian theories of fiction come closer to the actual operation of our understanding and enjoyment of fiction. But are Meinongian objects sufficiently differentiated? By taking objects of thought as paradigms and therefore defining objects as mere correspondents of sets of predicates, a Meinongian theory can neglect ontological differences other than those related to the regional origin of the object. The notion of *degree of being,* once eliminated from cosmology, may serve in the internal ontological models describing mythical and religious thought, and more generally symbolic activities of the mind. In Meinongian systems, every kind of object is equally endowed with being, although not necessarily with existence. A subtle distinction made by Meinong and used by Parsons suggests that for some of the extranuclear predicates there exist additional "watered-down" nuclear predicates corresponding to them: the extranuclear predicate "exists" would have a watered-down nuclear version, "is existent"; accordingly the golden mountain is existent but does not exist. Only real objects possess both the strong and the watered-down properties of existing and being existent.

A further enrichment of extranuclear predicates may be envisaged: "exists" could be construed as possessing several degrees of dilution, including symbolic existence. Meinongian theories call to our attention the presumptuousness of Russellian quantification over a universe of tangible objects: to scan the world and *not* to find Mr. Pickwick indicates a preliminary decision concerning certain symbolic entities and nonempirical beings. But an extension of ontology to realms beyond the borders of tangible reality requires a differentiated model: since, seen from the internal point of view of the users of fiction, Ryle's ontological no-man's-land turns out to be thickly settled, we must secure the means of describing the variegated, sometimes mutually exclusive communities that dwell in these vast areas. To be existent without existing is a sophisticated property equally shared by mathematical entities, unfinanced architectural monuments, spiritual emanations in gnostic systems, and fictional characters. We do not, however, want to see all nonempirical beings granted the same status; the ontology of fiction needs objects that look closer to those of the everyday universe than to mathematical entities and yet cannot be literally admitted to the real world, like unrealized projects and utopias. It is precisely the closeness of fiction to the empirical world that worries philosophers and contributes to what Richard Routley once called the "reality fixation" of analytical philosophy (1979, p. 4). But to reject segregationist policies does not suffice; a theory of fiction needs a differentiated internal outlook concerning fictional creatures, their properties and principles of individuation.

## Fictional Beings and the Causal Theory of Names

Hamlet, Anna Karenina, Sherlock Holmes, Macbeth's dagger, Des Esseintes' mansion, Proust's madeleine, are constantly talked about both by literary critics and by ordinary readers as if these characters and objects were fully individuated and, in some unspecified way, as if they empirically existed. At the same time, names like Anna Karenina and definite descriptions like Proust's madeleine do not denote in our world. In a detailed survey of various solutions for this puzzle, Robert Howell examines and rejects in turn several explanations, including an actualist Meinongian treatment of fictional objects, a proposal according to which fictional objects are nonactual but well-individuated entities existing in worlds different from ours, and a nonreferential view of such objects.[12] Among the reasons invoked by Howell against Parsons' Meinongian system, the most troubling casts doubts on the belief that to every distinct set of properties there corresponds a distinct, genuine object. The definition of objecthood in terms of sets of predicates leads to a metaphysics in which objects do not possess individuality other than numeric, since sets of properties can be shared by numerous objects, real or fictive. This crucial point surfaces again in Howell's rejection of the view that fictional objects are non-actual but well-individuated entities existing in alternative worlds. The discussion involves the causal theory of reference propounded by Saul Kripke, David Kaplan, Keith Donnellan, and Hilary Putnam.[13] According to this theory, for a name to refer to an object, there must be a way of uniquely specifying the object, independently of any contingent properties it may possess. Yet it seems impossible to identify Anna Karenina, Sherlock Holmes, and the rest otherwise than by the properties ascribed to them by the literary text. Therefore, Howell argues, since an indeterminate number of beings in various possible worlds may share these properties, there is no way of uniquely specifying Anna Karenina or Sherlock Holmes, which entails that everyday and fictional referring are again set widely apart.

Against Howell's view, and probably against the notions of the philosophers who proposed the causal theory as well, it seems to me that this theory, far from supporting the demarcation of fiction from actuality, in fact renders the integrationist view very plausible. To show this, it will be necessary to distinguish between two aspects of the causal theory and to claim that one of these aspects does not faithfully enough represent the practice of reference as it occurs in everyday discourse. I will also argue that reference to fictional characters and objects is not a logically strange activity, but rather that it relates to a common way of making reference.

To start, consider the following statements:

(1) John is just like Peter: neither can make a decision in due time.

(2) John is just like Hamlet: neither can make a decision in due time.

Statement (2) is a case of John Woods's mixed sentences, sentences that put together names of actual referents and names of fictional characters. How are these sentences to be understood? We might interpret sentence (1) as stating that John and Peter share the property of postponing their decisions, and sentence (2) as attributing this property to John and Hamlet. But, according to a widespread account, proper names are abbreviations of sets or clusters of definite descriptions. If so, the first sentence asserts that "John" and "Peter" abbreviate two sets of definite descriptions of certain entities, such that the description "$x$ cannot make decisions in due time" can be found in both sets.

The equivalence between names and sets of descriptions extends to fictional names as well, since it is conceivable that an artificial preparation of such a set be accompanied by a proper name attached to it: an author can imagine a set of properties: "lives in London," "is a bachelor," "is a dedicated student of human nature," and associate it with the name of Mr. Pickwick. Accordingly, sentence (2) may be understood as asserting that the same property figures in both sets of definite descriptions associated with the names of John and Hamlet. We are free to compare John and Hamlet despite the lack of denotation of the latter, since a standard Russellian representation of the sentence protects the user from unwanted ontological consequences.

However, not all mixed sentences are as easily dispensed with. Does Woods's sentence "Freud psychoanalyzed Gradiva" mean that the founder of psychoanalysis examined the set of definite descriptions that "Gradiva" stands for? Or how to read the next sentences?

(3)  Mary is in love with Jago.

(4)  Despite all she knew about Jago, Mary fell in love with him.

Criticizing the "abbreviation" theory of proper names, Kripke showed that these do not denote sets of properties but are rigid designators attached to individuals. A name imposed on a being refers to him even if the properties of this being are unknown, variable, or different from what one believes they are. "Shakespeare" is not the name of "whoever wrote *Hamlet* and *Othello*," since if one day irrefutable evidence is brought to light according to which these plays were written by, say, Francis Bacon, this discovery would not entail that Bacon *was* Shakespeare or that Shakespeare ceases to have been Shakespeare. Consequently, "Bacon" and "Shakespeare," and any other proper name, are linguistic labels pegged to individuals, independently of the properties displayed by these individuals.[14] This aspect of the causal theory of reference can be called the *structural* aspect. By showing that proper names cannot be identified with abbreviations of sets (or clusters) of definite descriptions, and by proposing the illuminating notion of proper names as rigid designators attached to some person or object, Kripke describes the structure of the relationship between the linguistic label and its bearer. Once attached to a being, a proper name refers to it, regardless of the possible changes in properties this being undergoes and *a fortiori* regardless of the changes in our knowledge of them. Insistence on the act of attaching names to beings constitutes the second, *historical* aspect of Kripke's theory of proper names. While the structural elements of the theory deal with the indexical nature of proper names, the historical aspect focuses on the operation of the imposition of names, which it assumes to be a historically identifiable act, involving an explicit decision and a clearly individuated object.

It is not difficult to see that the structural considerations proposed by the causal theory apply to fictional names as adequately as to ordinary proper names. "Hamlet" is not merely an abbreviation for a set of descriptions, since it can be naturally employed in counterfactual contexts. Our knowledge about this character can be modified without the name's being changed. One can say, for example:

(5) Had Hamlet married Ophelia, they would have lived happily ever after.

In the world where Hamlet marries Ophelia and lives happily ever after, he is still Hamlet and his bride is still Ophelia, in the same way in which, according to Kripke's arguments, if Napoleon had spent his entire life in Corsica he would still have been *himself*. The history of literature offers several examples of changes in literary works that have left the use of proper names unchanged. The eighteenth-century public could not accept the death of Cordelia in *King Lear* and preferred the modified version by Nahum Tate in which Cordelia survives and marries Edgar.[15] If a conjunction of properties defined proper names in fiction, Shakespeare's Cordelia would be a different individual from Tate's character. Although some aestheticians would probably want to claim this, the more common intuition is rather that Tate has not created a second Cordelia but has simply provided Cordelia with a happier destiny. The situation is comparable to cases when the original writer decides to change the destiny of a character or, better, with real-life reversals of destinies. "Being sentenced to death" suddenly ceased to belong to the set of descriptions of Feodor Dostoevsky, without entailing a change of his individuality. Even if one can say:

(6) Feodor is no more the person he was; his pardon changed him entirely.

this is understood to refer to his properties and behavior and not to his *identity*.

A possible objection to the extension of the causal theory to fictional names would consist in claiming that cases such as Cordelia's may be appropriately accommodated by the "cluster" version of the description theory. According to this version, a name is related to a cluster of properties, none of which is necessary for the name to apply. But the application of the name is correct only when at least an unspecified number of properties belonging to the cluster are present. Under this theory, the name "Cordelia" stands for a group of properties like "$x$ is Lear's younger daughter," "$x$ leads a French landing in Britain," "$x$ marries the king of France," "$x$ marries Edgar." Notice that the last two properties are incompatible, or at least they can be formulated so as to become incompatible. Yet this need not deter the proponents of the cluster theory, since a term like "game" may well be associated with a cluster of properties, some of which are mutually exclusive: "$x$ is played by two players" and "$x$ is played by four players." Accordingly, Tate's character may be properly called Cordelia, even if some of her properties are incompatible with those of the character in Shakespeare's play. But "Cordelia" will be nothing more than an abbreviation for a group of properties belonging to the cluster.

To counter this possible objection, one may point out that the paradigm case for the cluster theory is a group of exceptional cases, names like "game," "language," and so on, whose referents do not share a small group of essential features. As Putnam has convincingly argued, this situation does not necessarily extend to other types of names: names of natural kinds, for instance, cannot be treated as referring to clusters of descriptions. A generalization based on an idiosyncratic use of names does not necessarily fit the mainstream cases. What about proper names then? Kripke points out that in counterfactual statements all the properties belonging to the cluster, excepting a small group of individuating properties, may disappear, and yet the proper name may still be appropriately applied. Even if all the contingent properties of Aristotle were to change, he would still be the same person, if certain minimal requirements are met, such as, in Kripke's framework, the genetic structure of the fertilized egg that later became Aristotle. These minimal requirements for personal identity may of course vary according to the philosophical and scientific framework used. Medieval philosophy as well as writers like Alvin Plantinga today assume individuation to relate to a non-physical property, sometimes designated as *haecceity*, or individual essence. A theologian may consider that the central fact of individuation consists in God's associating a certain soul with the genetic structure. Ordinary use of language appears closer to individuation through haecceity or union between a body and a soul than to the biological constraint, for one can say with impunity:

(7) If Aristotle had different parents, he would have made a great king.

The implication is that Aristole could have been himself, even if his genetic structure were different. For a modern biologist to state such a sentence qua biologist would certainly be bizarre. Nevertheless, since not all of us are biologists, nothing prevents the layman from uttering or assenting to the above statement. Or consider a sentence like:

(8) If only I were the son of Rothschild.

Its utterer means that if *he,* as a well-individuated human being, were the son of Rothschild, *his* destiny would have been different. The sentence does not necessarily imply that were this wish fulfilled the *identity* of the speaker would be different (Williams, 1968). Although a reading bearing such an implication is not ruled out, the most common interpretation would assume the preservation of the speaker's identity in the world in which he indeed is Rothschild's son. Some philosophers would no doubt like to investigate the criteria of nonbiological, transworld identity. From the medieval theologian's point of view, there certainly is such a criterion. A phenomenologist may be equally ready to provide an intuitively acceptable nonbiological criterion.

Consequently, the cluster theory of names does not provide for an adequate representation of the use of proper names in actual situations. Philosophers who focus their discussion of names on actual and logically possible objects, while fully grasping this inadequacy, still appear to think that fictional names have to be treated differently from ordinary names, arguing that while names of actual and possible objects are not reducible to clusters of definite descriptions, names of fictional characters function precisely as abbreviations for such clusters. Mr. Pickwick's name, for instance, is exhausted by a cluster of properties described in Dickens' text or inferred by critics and readers. But against this distinction I must point out that, in the contexts of which I am aware, the reasons for the difference in treatment are always *historical.* Structurally the use of "Cordelia" is not distinct from that of "Aristotle" or "Socrates." Indeed, let us assume that

Nahum Tate wrote a play in which Cordelia is capable, from the outset, of expressing her love for her father, does not marry the king of France but accompanies Lear through his tribulations, and marries Edgar in the end. Literary critics possessing some degree of sophistication would probably claim that Tate replaced Cordelia by another character. Still, the most common way of describing what happened is to say that in Tate's hypothetical play Cordelia behaves differently than *she* does in Shakespeare's play. To make the argument intuitively clearer, let us imagine a play in which there are many vague allusions to a character named Ugolo. Ugolo never appears on stage, he is not related to any of the actions, and no one knows anything precise about him. The characters make sudden remarks like "Mary, think of Ugolo!" or "John, don't forget Ugolo," or "Often in bed, before going to sleep, I remember Ugolo." The descriptions related to this name are obscure and noncommittal; they could not possibly serve as identifying descriptions in Donnellan's sense. Still, before long, the spectators know that there is some entity, called Ugolo, who (which?) has precisely the only property that nobody knows of any of his (its?) properties. Assume now that in a second play one learns that Ugolo is a half-mad dwarf kept prisoner in an underground cell; suppose moreover that he manages to escape and makes a triumphant entrance on stage. The spectators who have seen the first play will be relieved to flesh out Ugolo. But that Ugolo had some identity, even if entirely undetermined from an epistemic point of view, they already knew from the indications supplied by the first play.

The Ugolo example attempts to show that fictional characters can be named and individuated independently of any kind of description. The way the name Ugolo works is not unlike any rigid designator, although it is perfectly true that there is no means of uniquely specifying its bearer in the actual world. Consequently, fictional names are not used as abbreviations for either conjunctions or clusters of definite descriptions. The practice of writers, critics, and ordinary people speaking about fictional characters and objects rather suggests that within fiction names work like usual proper names, that is as rigid designators attached to individuated objects, independent of the objects' properties. Insofar as the structural aspects are concerned, there is no detectable difference between nonfictional and fictional proper names.

As for the historical component of the causal theory of reference, it does not decisively affect the assumption that fictional names designate well-individuated entities. The causal theory assumes that reference is determined by an initial act of imposing a name on a referent. How exactly the *impositio nominis* takes place is not entirely clear. Kripke's, Kaplan's, and Donnellan's papers suggest that a name can be attached only to a *uniquely specified* object. The unique specification appears to be of an empirical nature: one of Kripke's much discussed examples features the astronomer Leverrier who, after discovering some abnormalities in the orbit of the planet Uranus, figured out that they were caused by the presence of an undiscovered planet and decided to call the planet Neptune. An example offered by Kaplan and slightly modified by Donnellan stipulates that provided the first child born in the twenty-first century will in fact exist, his name can be fixed now as, say, "Newman 1." It may have turned out that the abnormalities of Uranus were caused by some other factor than the unknown planet; in the same vein it is not inconceivable that there will be no children born in the twenty-first century. In both cases, then, the names "Neptune" and "Newman 1" would be rigid designators of objects that turn out not to exist. However, they rigidly designate uniquely specifiable objects in possible worlds that bear a relationship of empirical alternativeness to the actual world. The unique specification and the empirical possibility of the *denominatum* are obligatory conditions for an *impositio nominis* to be acceptably established.

Conversely, when faced with a name, one might decide whether its reference is acceptably established, by causally or historically retracing the actual use to the original *impositio nominis*. Thus, the name "Glenn Gould" referring to the well-known pianist is acceptably used in a piece of conversation if one is theoretically able to go backwards in time in a step-by-step fashion, so as to relate the association between the name and the referent to an original baptism. This requirement is intended to rule out situations in which a proper name is mistakenly used. Suppose that someone who is listening to a recording of the *Well-Tempered Clavier* praises Glenn Gould's performance when in fact the pianist is, say, Sviatoslav Richter. By checking step by step the origin of the recording and the name of the pianist back to the original baptism, one would find a Richter baptism rather than a Gould one. The chain of relations between the baptism and the actual use needs not be made up only of strictly causal relations, as Donnellan points out. It is sufficient that a clear historical sequence link the two moments.

Based on this procedure, Donnellan argues that in order for a statement containing a proper name to be true or false, an individual is required who relates historically to the use of his name. For the statement

(9)   Homer was a great poet

to have a truth value, one must be able to locate an individual, correctly related to the use of the name "Homer" by a chain of historical links. If such an individual is not found, there will be a failure of reference. The statement

(10)   Homer did not exist

is true, according to Donnellan, "just in case there is a failure of reference, not in the statement itself, but in other possible or actual predicative statements involving the name," such as (9) above. What constitutes, then, a failure of reference? In order to answer this question, Donnellan examines an example involving fictional beings. A child who discovers that Santa Claus is a fiction and states

(11)   Santa Claus does not exist

means that sentences like "Santa Claus comes tonight" are cases of reference failure. What happens is that by checking historically the origin of the name "Santa Claus," the child finds an *event* that precludes any referent being identified, namely the fact that Santa Claus was introduced into her language through a fiction told her by adults. Donnellan calls such events "blocks" in the referential history of names. Other examples of blocks include situations in which a child invents imaginary companions with whom she pretends to converse, or the instance in which, although Homeric poems were in fact composed by many different writers, at some point an ancient scholar attributed them to a single person, called "Homer." Nonexistent beings are those whose referential history ends in a block; fictional beings are introduced through blocks as well.

But think of a Greek city, say Athens, where myths were strongly believed in. From the internal point of view of fifth-century Athenians, names like Zeus, Aphrodite, or Pallas Athena referred to well-individuated beings, full of interesting properties, beings who intervened in daily lives, who had to be addressed and appeased. For members of that community, the name Pallas Athena worked as a rigid designator, attached to an individual deity, uniquely specifiable according to a set of criteria (Pallas Athena was *the* goddess who protected Athens, *the* daughter of Zeus, born in a special way by emerging from his head, and so on), criteria that were acceptable within the given community. In a twentieth-century external account, one is justified to claim that the citizens of Athens in the fifth century lived in a perpetual state of reference failure. However, from the point of view of the *users,* their speaker's references, in Kripke's sense, to gods and goddesses were entirely successful.[16] Yet, and in spite of their success, no one would have been able to point to a correct (in Donnellan's sense) chain of historical links relating the uses of godly names to earlier baptisms. Instead, everyone took for granted that the myths about the origins of the gods provided for a particularly reliable source of name assignments. Putnam's views on the division of linguistic labor can help us again here: according to him, contemporary people may speak about objects they would not know how to recognize, because in the society as a whole there are specialists who can solve the more difficult cases: thus one can use the term "gold" and be ignorant of the chemical tests for its recognition because, if the need arose, experts would decide. But suppose there is a country isolated from outside technology and in which the people are no longer capable of telling whether something is really gold. Would this mean that the population of that country should stop *speaking* of gold? They may continue to refer to gold, reassured by the memory of happier times when goldsmiths were still around to verify whether some piece of yellow metal was gold or not.

A similar situation might arise in a religious city. Its citizens may admit that no one has seen the gods for some time; the myths, however, are taken to be the memories of those who, many years earlier, still lived in the company of gods. After a certain period of time, belief in particular gods might wane. There is no unique cause for this phenomenon: people are exposed to foreign religions and acquire a sense of religious relativity, philosophers offer new alternatives based on abstract reasoning, new religions subvert the old ones. It is therefore hard to assume that collective (or individual) loss of faith in a given mythology can always be represented as a discovery that, at some point in the historical links relating the names of gods to the initial imposing of names, there has been a block, or an event that mistakenly introduced these names as rigid designators of existing entities. More likely, the mythology *as a whole* starts gradually to lose its credibility. In the history of weakening mythologies, often there is a period of systematic ambiguity, when people cannot commit themselves to the literal existence of most gods and their traditional feats without this entailing a radical negation of the existence of some gods in subtler forms than those narrated by the myths. At this stage the myths about the surviving gods are interpreted symbolically as saying something nonliteral about existing and probably well-individuated gods.

The mythological mind is said to distinguish between at least three kinds of statements: factual statements, which cover everyday life, true statements, referring to gods and heroes, and fictions, which include stories other than myths (fables, funny moral stories). Differences between these statements are not always clear, since in many societies factual statements are closely related to the mythical ones. The distinction between mythical truth, which is assumed to be more profound and serious than factual truth, and leisure-oriented fiction is, however, well established. When a mythological system gradually loses its grip on a society, the ancient gods and heroes start to be perceived as fictional characters. But can we equate the suspension of religious belief with the discovery of a block, of an *event* that in ancient times made people assume that gods were real? Would it not be more likely that the block is set precisely when the mythological system gradually ceases to be a religious truth and slowly slides into fiction? And is it not more probable that this block or warning device is (figuratively) installed at the *entrance* into the newly fictionalized domain than at the origins of the historical links relating each name of a god to the god's baptism? What happens in such cases is that with the weakening of the mythological system, one or more or all individuals belonging to that mythology is (are) moved into another domain. But if an individual or an entire population of supernatural beings bearing names, having properties, slides into fiction, does it mean that its members lose their internal individuation and status as beings?

That from a structural point of view proper names are rigid designators does not entail that historically their attachment to entities is always recovered through a backward chain of causal or historical links, at least in the sense of contemporary factually oriented theories. Humans largely use names and mean them as rigid designators, without paying much attention to the corresponding causal and historical chains, even or perhaps especially when such chains have misty origins. Requirements concerning causal or historical chains of reference should thus be relaxed and relativized to the different referential practices of the various speech communities (Evans, 1973). In addition, referential practice suggests that in dealing with mythology, religion, and fiction it is useful to set up an internal model, involving different domains, populated by different kinds of beings. Blocks are thus rendered unnecessary: what they are supposed to explain should be represented by the *moving* of an individual from one domain to the other; as a consquence of the allowance for travel between domains, real and fictional, the representation of mixed sentences would become less problematic.

This amounts to a plea for richer models that include realms different from the actual world. The constitution of such models would allow the theory of fiction to look for explanations beyond the level of fictional individuals. As shown above, fictional beings do not necessarily come into existence through individual gates or blocks in their referential history; rather, their fate is linked with the movements of populous groups that share the same ontological destiny. Fictionality cannot be understood as an individual feature: it encompasses entire realms of beings. The theory of fiction must thus turn to fictional worlds.

# 3 ⁓ Salient Worlds

I N THE previous chapter I distinguished between an external approach to fiction, which aims at gauging it against the nonfictional world, and an internal approach whose purpose is to propose models representing the user's understanding of fiction. The internal approach needs a conceptual framework more relaxed than the segregationist approach. Nor should reflections on fiction limit themselves to a theory of fictional discourse; a richer system, perhaps related to Meinongian ontologies, would render better service to the poetics of fiction. Although the attention of segregationist and Meinongian philosophers alike has mostly been directed toward a theory of fictional objects, important cultural intuitions link these objects into fictional worlds. Now I shall examine in more detail this notion, by presenting some of the concepts used in modal semantics and attempting to explore their use in an internal theory of fiction; a criticism of the notion of possible worlds applied to fiction will then lead to a typology of worlds, imaginary or not, pointing the way to a flexible definition of fictionality.

## Possible Worlds

A difficulty shared by classical segregationism and Meinongian theories is their inability to discriminate between various kinds of inactuality. To assert that Mr. Pickwick is wise is quite different from claiming that if George VI had had a first-born son he would have made a wise king. If the domain of true discourse coincides with that of actuality, both statements will be discarded as false or spurious; conversely, a theory that accepts with firm liberality all nonexistent entities will equally miss the difference between mere fiction and unrealized possibility.[1] To avoid such undesirable confusion, we may turn to modal semantics, since it proposes a representation of possibility and necessity that allows truth and falsity to apply to statements about nonactual entities and situations.

A *model structure* in Saul Kripke's sense is a logical construction consisting of a set K of elements, a well-designated member G of this set, and a relation R between the elements of the set.[2] Under an interpretation influenced by Leibniz' notion of *possible world,* the set K may be viewed as a set of possible worlds, the privileged member G as the real world, and the relation R as the link between various worlds belonging to the system K and their possible alternatives within K. To establish a relation of alternativeness from one world to the next, one needs a criterion—say the identity of the individuals who populate the worlds. We may say that a world belonging to the set K represents a possible alternative to some other world from the same system if the first world includes the same inventory of individuals as the second, even if some of the properties of these individuals undergo changes. Imagine a world H identical with the world G in which we live, except for the fact that in G some individuals live in Montreal, while in H they have moved to Toronto. The list of individuals belonging to G is exactly the same as the list of individuals in H; the only change involves properties of these individuals. Defined in his way, the relation R stipulates that world H is a possible alternative to our world G. Conversely, if J is a world partially identical with G but containing only half of the present population of G, then, according to our criterion, J is not an alternative to G. Since each world has the same individuals as itself, more generally, since every world is an alternative to itself, the relation R is called reflexive.

The relation R can be modified so as to include other criteria of alternativeness as well. Imagine a world I that is accessible from G, the converse being false. Temporal succession is a simple case of asymmetric accessibility: with a bit of patience and some luck we may reach the world of January 1987, having as a starting point the world of January 1986, but the converse is impossible. Accessibility and alternativeness formally represent the intuition that some states of affairs are possible relative to the real ones while others are not. We have access to possible alternatives but are cut off from impossible worlds.

The model structure is supplemented with a model that assigns each atomic proposition a truth value in each world belonging to the system. In agreement with Leibniz' logic, propositions that are true not only in the actual world but in all possible worlds as well will be called necessary truths; conversely, a proposition is possible in our real world, if it is true in at least one possible world accessible from ours. The model structure becomes a quantificational model structure if one adds to it a function that assigns to each world a set of individuals called the *domain* of the world in question. The domains of different worlds belonging to the system K are not necessarily identical: a world H that is possible relative to the actual world G may contain more or less individuals than G, unless, of course, the relation R is so defined as to link only worlds that share the same domain.

Sometimes it is interesting to define the relation R so as to connect the real world G with some of the worlds belonging to the system K, but not necessarily with all of them. If such is the case, the system K will be partitioned into two subsystems: the set K' of worlds accessible from G, and the set K'' of worlds inaccessible from G. It is easy to imagine some world F belonging to the set K'' of worlds inaccessible from G and bearing the relation R to some other members of K, such that although F is not a possible alternative of G, there are plenty of worlds that are accessible *from F*.

As to the status of individuals in this system, we have already seen that a function attributes a domain of individuals to each world in the set K. For simplicity, the function can be considered as defined in the actual world; we thus possess an inventory of the individuals (objects, constants) that exist in the initial real world. The situation becomes more problematic when considering the possible alternatives of the actual world: how can we define a function that attributes individuals to possible worlds? This question is a modern version of an old philosophical problem: "does everything that exists necessarily exist?" Modal logicians and philosophers have debated the consequences of an affirmative answer to this question. It is obvious from the metaphysical as well as from the logical point of view that it makes a serious difference if we postulate that possible worlds must have the same inventory of individuals as the real world, or if we allow worlds accessible from ours to contain fewer individuals or more.

This question has interesting consequences in the theory of fiction: it is perhaps not entirely by chance that, in the very paper that lays the foundation of modal semantics, Kripke exemplifies possibility by making use of a fictional being: "Sherlock Holmes," he asserts, "doesn't exist, but in other states of affairs he would have existed." As Kripke's remark indicates, to require from possible worlds an inventory of beings identical to the inventory of the actual one is a position too restrictive for the representation of fictional ontologies. If all possible worlds must display the same domain of individuals as the real world, then a world that includes new individuals is not possible relative to the actual world. But this is not only counterintuitive in every day discourse, in which the existence, for instance, of unborn relatives is assumed to be a genuine possibility, but also in our usual understanding of fictional texts. Kripke's assertion about Sherlock Holmes is based on a common aesthetic intuition that takes for granted that things found in novels are in some way compatible with real life. A semantic system that intends to take this intuition into account has to show tolerance toward new individuals, such as Sherlock Holmes. Indeed, since Kripke's semantics allows the inventory of individuals to vary from one domain to the other, which means that it allows individuals who do not actually exist to belong to some world accessible from our real world, why not accept that Sherlock Holmes, who does not belong to the set of individuals of our world, would have existed in other states of affairs? Aristotle maintains that "it is not the poet's business to tell what happened, but the kind of things that would happen—what is possible according to possibility and necessity" (*Poetics* IX.1). In other words, the poet must put forward either propositions true in every alternative of the real world (things possible according to necessity) or propositions true at least in one alternative of the actual world (things possible according to probability). Moreover, as Aristotle notices, the tragic poets "keep to real people." When Shakespeare writes the tragedy of Julius Caesar, he uses characters that belong to the actual world. Is it not natural to think that if, owing to an unpleasant accident of history, Sherlock Holmes does not happen to have existed, he would have existed in another state of affairs?

It is worth noting that this is not merely philosophical speculation related to the transfer of possible-world semantics to the worlds of fiction. There are many real historical and social settings in which writers and their public accept the assumption that a literary work speaks of something that is genuinely possible relative to the real world. This attitude corresponds to realist literature, in the broad sense of the term. Seen from this angle, realism is not merely a set of stylistic and narrative conventions, but a fundamental attitude toward the relationship between the actual world and the truth of literary texts. In a realist perspective, the criterion of the truth and falsity of a literary text and of its details is based upon the notion of possibility (and not only *logical* possibility) with respect to the actual world. Different kinds of realism vary, of course, according to the description of the actual world and to the definition of the relation R that connects this world to its possible alternatives. The actual world as well as the relation of accessibility are different for the authors of medieval miracle plays compared to the author of a modern mystery novel. A world in which the statue of the Virgin Mary speaks to a layman belongs to the range of possibility for a medieval writer and his public, just as a world in which an FBI narcotics squad dismantles a network of drug dealers and arrests everybody is a possible world for the writer of a contemporary mystery novel and its readers. In spite of the variations, these two cases share the same logical attitude toward the information conveyed by literary discourse and its relationships to the actual world.

Inventories of individuals are by no means the only area in which the logic that underlies writing and understanding fiction displays similarities with modal logic. Imagine a possible world H and a very large, possibly infinite set P$h$ of propositions true therein. Imagine also an ideal reader for whom H is the only possible alternative of the actual world G, which means that for this speaker propositions true in H are possible in G. Notice that the set P$h$ being very large, the reader knows only a small part of it; consequently, when confronted with a proposition $p$ which he does not yet know, he has to decide whether or not $p$ is likely to belong to the set P$h$ of propositions true in the world H (and consequently possible in the actual world G). Let us assume that the reader is provided with an intuitive decision procedure that allows him to find out within a reasonable period of time whether or not proposition $p$ belongs to the set P$h$. If the reader decides that $p$ is true in H (hence possible in G), $p$ is said to have been integrated into P$h$. The situation is slightly more complex when the actual world G has more than one alternative world in the system K. In this case, one can say that a new proposition $p$ is integrated into P$c$, C being the set of possible worlds that belong to K and are accessible from G, if $p$ is integrated in at least one member of the set C. If $p$ is considered as true in the actual world G, one can say that $p$ is accepted by the reader. Accepted is thus synonymous with integrated into the set P$g$ of sentences true in the real world.

A reader, for instance, finds in his trustworthy newspaper that a team of researchers has landed on Mars. He diligently accepts the information, which means that he integrates it into the set P$g$ of sentences true in our actual world. Suppose, however, that the newspaper does not speak about the fact of the landing on Mars, but only reports on rumors circulating in well-informed circles and predicting the imminent beginning of a secret mission to that planet. In this case, the reader must use his decision procedure in order to see if he can integrate the new information in at least one world H compatible with the actual world G. Remembering that space research can be used for military purposes, and that for security reasons some missions are kept secret, our reader may succeed in imagining a likely state of affairs that results in a secret landing on Mars; therefore he integrates the news in the set P$c$. If, on the contrary, the news contradicts too forcibly what he knows about space research, he will decide not to integrate the news into P$c$ and will think: "Impossible!"

The logic of understanding a novel does not work differently. Instead of a newspaper suppose that our reader examines a novel, say *La Princesse de Clèves* by Madame de La Fayette, and attempts to decide whether the propositions constained in it can or cannot be integrated into P$c$. The beginning of the novel—"Magnificence and gallantry had never appeared in France with such brilliance as in the last years of the reign of Henry II"—may easily be integrated into the set of possible truths P$c$ and even into the set of actual truths P$g$. The same thing holds for the next sentences of the novel, even if the reader may become more hesitant when the author, after having introduced characters whose historical existence is familiar, proceeds to the less-authenticated characters and introduces the fictional heroine. But such hesitation does not affect the logical procedure, since the reader does not have only to signal the propositions accepted into P$g$ and therefore assumed to be true in the actual world G, but also to indicate the propositions integrated into P$c$, that is, the propositions possible in G.

Yet, despite the striking parallelisms in the logic of their understanding, fiction cannot be strictly identified with metaphysically possible worlds. Arguing against such an identification, Howell noticed that it may lead us to assume the existence of fictional worlds, together with the fictional objects they contain, independent of the novelist who describes them. But, Howell argues, this would entail the implausible conclusion that the author, Dickens for instance, did not create Mr. Pickwick but rather "identified" him by inspecting the possible world to which the gentle bachelor belongs. Moreover, a possible-world approach would not account for contradictory fictions: the skillful Sherlock Holmes may draw a square circle, in which case his world would cease being a technically possible world (1979, pp. 137–140). Notice that a Meinongian account would not have this difficulty, since Meinongian objects can be associated with any set of properties, including contradictory sets.

Howell's argument warns us against a literal understanding of the notion of possible world in the context of fiction. If possible worlds existed somewhere in a mysterious hyperspace, then indeed it would go against our intuitions to assume that Dickens just obtained access of the cluster of Pickwick-worlds and faithfully described them. At least one philosopher of modal logic, David Lewis, has defended the view that all possible worlds, together with all the objects that populate them, are as real as our own world.[3] But this form of possibilism is an extreme position, which offends our most common intuitions. Usually philosophers assume that possible worlds are not genuine concrete entities that could be inspected were we to possess the adequate telescope; they are abstract models, and may be thought of either as actual abstract entities or as conceptual constructions.[4] But if so, the relation between a world and its creator matters less; to represent works of fiction as worlds involves a model that does not necessarily include a rigorous theory of the production of the fictional world: in this, the model reassembles the usual activity of the reader who can contemplate the world of Mr. Pickwick independently of who established it and when, leaving aside the inquiry about the process of creation. Besides, literary history favors this attitude, since in addition to the modern cases in which the author can be said to have created the fictional world (or at least major parts of it), there are innumerable instances in which much of this world preexists, and the writer more or less faithfully "identifies" and describes it: plays on mythological topics and neoclassical tragedies patterned after Greek or Roman texts are examples that first come to mind.

The image of Sherlock Holmes drawing square circles undisturbed by geometric constraints is nonetheless worrisome, since contradictory objects indeed occur in fiction, sometimes only marginally but sometimes centrally, as in Borges' metaphysical stories or in contemporary science fiction. The presence of contradictions effectively prevents us from considering fictional worlds as genuine possible worlds and from reducing the theory of fiction to a Kripkean theory of modality. Contradictory objects nevertheless provide insufficient evidence against the notion of *world,* since nothing prevents the theory of fiction from speaking, as some philosophers do, about impossible or erratic worlds. Contradictory worlds are not so remote as one might expect. Not only is physics still divided between the theory of relativity and quantum mechanics, not only is light simultaneously made up of particles and waves, but also our everyday worlds host such impossible entities as individual psyches, desires, dreams, and symbols. Consistent worlds originate in a strong idealization, and our commitment to coherence is less warranted than it appears. After all, humans lived in notoriously incongruous universes long before these became more or less cohesive. Nineteenth-century realist novels may have aimed at constructing genuine possible alternatives to the actual world, as filtered through the modern scientific episteme; but this ambition did not last long, and in order to obtain novel aesthetic and cognitive effects, contemporary literature often posits worlds as impossible as the most archaic ones. Kripkean modal semantics offers what could be called a *distant* model for the theory of fiction: rather than a rigorously unified semantics, fiction needs a typology of worlds to represent the variety of fictional practice. And if, on the one hand, technically impeccable possible worlds are too narrowly defined to provide for a model in the theory of fiction, on the other hand the notion of world as an ontological metaphor for fiction remains too appealing to be dismissed.[5] An attempt should be made at relaxing and qualifying this crucial notion.

## Worlds and Books about Them, a First Approach

Possible worlds can be understood as abstract collections of states of affairs, distinct from the statements describing those states, distinct thereby from the complete list of sentences kept in the *book about the world*. In Alvin Plantinga's view, a possible world defines "a way things could have been . . . a possible state of affairs of some kind"(1974, p. 44). In our world, states of affairs may obtain, or be actual, but they may also not obtain. Thus, *Julius Caesar's dying as a consequence of the wounds inflicted by the conspirators* is an actual state of affairs, as opposed to *Julius Caesar's surviving the plot against his life*. The latter qualifies as a possible state of affairs, under the constraints of human biology, while *Julius Caesar's living for two thousand years* does not. A state of affairs like *Julius Caesar's having squared the circle* is impossible in a stronger sense, since it not only presupposes a change in the laws of nature but a modification of the laws of logic as well. Plantinga understands possible worlds as states of affairs that (1) do not violate the laws of logic, broadly understood; (2) are maximal or complete. To characterize completeness, he defines *inclusion* as follows: a state of affairs S includes another state of affairs S' if S cannot obtain without S' obtaining as well. Thus, *Julius Caesar's dying as a consequence of the wounds inflicted by the conspirators* includes *The conspirators wounding Julius Caesar*. Conversely, a state of affairs S precludes another state of affairs S' if S obtains only if S' fails to obtain. For instance, *Julius Caesar's dying as a consequence of the wounds inflicted by the conspirators* precludes *The conspiracy against Caesar having been canceled*. A maximal state of affairs S is such that for any state S' it either includes or precludes it. The actual world obviously is a maximal state of affairs in Plantinga's sense; it is the only possible world that obtains.

Consider next the following proposition:

(1) Socrates is snubnosed

as intimately related to the state of affairs

(2) Socrates' being snubnosed.

Plantinga argues that since it is impossible for (1) to be true without (2) obtaining, and vice-versa, (1) entails (2) and (2) entails (1). For any possible world W, he continues, "the *book on W* is the set B of propositions such that *p* is a member of B if W entails *p*." Thus only propositions entailed by corresponding states of affairs in the world belong to the book on that world. In Plantinga's account, books are tightly linked to worlds: to each world corresponds one and only one book. Since his definition of worlds makes use of maximality or completeness, books also will be maximal: for any proposition *p*, the book B on W will contain either *p* or its negation *non-p*. The book on the actual world will therefore either contain *Julius Caesar died as a consequence of the wounds inflicted by the conspirators* or its negation, *It is not true that Julius Caesar died as a consequence of the wounds inflicted by the conspirators*. A book on a world W is a complete list of propositions true in that world.

Now a modal theory needs to consider worlds not only in isolation but clustered in universes as well. Let us define a universe U in the Kripkean spirit as a set K of worlds, an actual world belonging to K, and a relation R of alternativeness. The universe includes an actual world and many other worlds, some of which are accessible from the actual by virtue of the relation R. Each universe thus possesses its own actual world, which can be called its *base*. A universe will host a constellation of the worlds around a base; clearly, the same base can be surrounded by more than one universe. The relation R will be allowed to cover different conceptions of possibility: logical, metaphysical, psychological, and so on. Notice that the definition of the universe does not include a maximality requirement.

The true sentences about the entire universe are collected in the set of books about each of its worlds. We may give this set the name of *Magnum Opus* on U, and reserve its First Book for the true sentences in the base or actual world of the universe. Another volume, which could be called the Book of Rules, would include higher-order considerations about the universe, its worlds and their books, explanations of the ways in which the relation R links the worlds of the universe U, or hints concerning the nature of the language used in the *Magnum Opus*.

For it is not self-evident that all *Magna Opera* should or even could be couched in the same language. Differences between properties of the worlds of various universes may well require a differentiation of the language describing them. Thus, to speak about a universe containing colors, one needs a language that possesses qualitative predicates. Moreover, one should consider the possibility that the same universe could be described by different *Magna Opera* using different languages. As pointed out during recent discussions in philosophy of science and mind, phenomena accounted for by various disciplines articulate only approximately with one another, each level of study enjoying a certain independence: the structure of the world appears thus to possess an irreducible plasticity, such that there is no privileged vantage point from which to direct the organization of knowledge definitively.[6] Supposing that all science speaks about the same world, ours, it follows that the real universe will have to be discussed in many different books and *Magna Opera*. This is not just a de facto situation, attributable to the limited state of our knowledge about the world; on the contrary, the nature of knowledge is such that since each particular science strives to fill its own First Book, or its own *Magnum Opus* with true sentences about the real world and its genuine alternatives, these books and opera will never form a single, compact *Magnum Opus* but will instead coexist as various descriptions of the same universe. The picture is further complicated by the indeterminacy of reference, as described by Quine (1969) and generalized to possible worlds by Putnam (1981, pp. 32–35). These authors show that given a certain theory, and *a fortiori* a certain text, its reference cannot be unambiguously specified in a given world or set of worlds. The same text can equally well refer to an infinity of distinct worlds. Plantinga's one-to-one relation between worlds and books has to give way to a more complex configuration, in which one universe can be associated with more than one *Magnum Opus,* and the same *Magnum Opus* can serve as the description of more than one universe.

These complications undermine linguistic optimism. The principle of expressibility (Searle, 1969, pp. 19–21), according to which any content can appropriately be expressed by some linguistic means, may not always apply. For, if the links between universes, *Magnum Opera,* and languages are more diversified, it becomes a distinct possibility that a certain universe falls outside the scope of a certain language, and therefore of any *Magnum Opus* couched in that language. An idiom containing a finite number of constants and no variables cannot describe a universe displaying an infinite number of beings; a language lacking quality predicates will prove inadequate for a universe containing colors. When such situations arise, I shall call the universe in question *indescribable* with respect to the language; clearly, a universe may be indescribable with respect to some language L$i$ but could be adequately portrayed in some other language L$j$.[7]

Some universes, moreover, may be radically indescribable, in the sense that as they appear to their inhabitants, they could not be accounted for in any existing or imaginable language. In order to qualify as radically indescribable, a universe need not be indescribable in every respect: it may display just one region that cannot be grasped by any language. The paradigm case is the universe containing a God about whom one cannot speak adequately; the universe, that is, referred to by various trends of mystic and negative theology. If God is such that no attribute is suitable to him and if, as theologians assert, it is equally true that God exists and that he does not, then, from an internal perspective, the universe structured around God is radically indescribable at its very core.[8] Any *Magnum Opus* describing it from such a perspective would be irremediably faulty. The principle of expressibility, therefore, appears to exclude a certain number of cases. Besides expressible universes, there may exist *ultra-Meinongian* universes, comprising beings or states of affairs about which it is impossible for their inhabitants to speak in any suitable way. Someone who accepts the principle of expressibility can of course argue that the entire population of an ultra-Meinongian universe is wrong, since the notion of a god about whom one cannot adequately speak in any conceivable language does not make sense. In turn, the inhabitants could well ask: "Sense for *whom?*" If the expressibility principle presupposes certain philosophical opinions, does this not mean that its application is limited?

But then approached internally, the difference between fictional and nonfictional semantics loses some of its bluntness. The distinction between the two appears to be one of degree rather than nature.

Similarly to *Magna Opera* about the actual universe, the reference of fictional texts is in principle indeterminate; like various theories each positing its own level of actuality, fiction employs a multiplicity of bases, of worlds "actual"-in-the-system. *Don Quixote's* universe develops around a basic level that is different both from our actuality and from the world described by, say, *Persiles and Sigismunda* or *The Pickwick Papers.* Conversely, just as the real world is the object of a variety of books and *Magna Opera,* fictional worlds fail to exert a monopoly over their books. To assume that *Don Quixote's* universe could have been described by another book or opus than that represented by Cervantes' text may sound blasphemous. But in a broader perspective there are no convincing arguments against the possibility of relating various books and opera to the same fictional base. The universe of Greek gods and heroes was not invented anew by Aeschylus, Sophocles, and Euripides; instead each developed a certain language or a certain angle of vision in relation to a relatively stable mythological universe. And did not the world of Quixote become the object of Avellaneda's plagiarism, to the point that Cervantes was forced to assert his monopoly on it?

## Games of Make-Believe: Dual Structures

Universes, together with their *Magna Opera,* thus offer internal models for both reality and fiction. The least elaborate internal model is a simple or flat structure, composed of just one universe containing a base, the actuality, surrounded by its aura of genuinely possible alternatives. To appreciate fully the compactness of simple structures, one should consider that they allow for no alternative base or for any movement outside the given actuality and its constellation of possibilities. Moreover, a given object that belongs to such a structure is ontologically "locked in" and cannot change its status or be assigned a different nature and function in some other structure, because there is no such structure. Ironically, since we tend to cluster universes and to link them to one another in complex constructions, it is not easy to find an example of a flat structure. But think of a world in which children could not pretend that globs of mud of a certain shape and size are pies, or that tree stumps are bears, because neither the globs of mud nor the tree stumps can be taken as anything but what they are. The idea would never cross the minds of the inhabitants that the constituents of their universe can be used as building blocks for a different kind of world, in which they may acquire new ontological traits. Seen from an external perspective, a flat structure is therefore a model representing the attitude of a population entirely deprived of the faculty of imagination.

As things stand, a population deprived of imagination is but one person's fantasy in a population endowed with imagination. An internal model striving to represent the current practices of human communities would therefore need more elaborate constructions. To clarify the kind of phenomena such a model should be expected to account for, we might take as a departure point Kendall Walton's theory of fictional entities.[9] In Walton's view, "the central metaphysical issue of the ontological status of fictional entities is embodied in the experience of being *caught up in a story*" (1984, p. 179). When immersed in the adventures of Anna Karenina, even if we do not actually believe what Tolstoy's text tells us, we let ourselves "be convinced, momentarily and partially, at least, of the existence of Anna Karenina and of the truth of what is said about her in the novel." This happens, Walton argues, because works of fiction are not mere sequences of sentences but props in a *game of make-believe,* like children playing with dolls or pretending to be cowboys. The reader who accepts that Anna Karenina is unhappy or that she loves Vronsky recognizes that such propositions are true in the world of that game. And just as children pretending to feed dolls that in the game are (fictionally) babies become themselves fictional moms and dads fictionally feeding their offspring, readers of *Anna Karenina* who cry at the character's tragic end fictionally attend Anna's suicide, that is participate (as spectators) in a game of make-believe. And rather than assuming that the readers of *Anna Karenina* contemplate a fictional world from some privileged vantage point outside it, Walton insists that the readers are located *within* the fictional world that, for the duration of the game, is taken as real. Developing Walton's analysis, Gareth Evans sketches a set of principles that govern games of make-believe. The basic principles stipulate a set of make-believe truths. In a mud-pie game, for instance, a few such principles are in force:

(1)  Globs of mud fashioned into pie-shape will be taken as pies.

(2)  Small black pebbles will be taken as raisins.

(3)  A metal object will be taken as a hot oven.

An incorporation principle allows for the addition to the game of any truth not ruled out by the basic principles ("Mary likes raisin pies"), while a recursive principle governs the construction of new make-believe truths from the basic principles and the incorporated truths. To extend the analysis to a work of fiction, one may think of a theatrical performance: actors will be taken as King Lear, Gloucester, Cornwall, Albany, Kent, Cordelia; the stage will be taken as Lear's palace, Gloucester's castle, the French camp at Dover; the words pronounced by the performers will be taken as Lear's, Gloucester's, and so on. Various truths concerning the world and the spectators' beliefs and intentions can be incorporated into the game, and new propositions can be formed with their help.

Now when a group of children play with mud, they simultaneously touch globs of mud—in the really real world—*and* offer one another tasty pies in the world of make-believe, which is real within the game. Running away from tree stumps in the real world becomes, for the same children, a flight from dangerous bears in the world of make-believe. An objective spectator of these games would know that since there are no tasty pies or dangerous bears, the children only *make it fictional of themselves* (to use Walton's expression) that they serve one another delicious pies or that they flee from ferocious bears. Similarly, we know quite well that in terms of the really real world the king on stage is just an actor, his palace a painted piece of cardboard, and his words a sequence of lines invented long ago by an English poet. If, however, we want not so much to explain away the illusion generated by the game of make-believe and express what happens in terms of the really real world, as to account for our participation during such games, in both the really real world and the fictionally real worlds, we must distinguish between the two distinct levels on which the game takes place and show the links between them.

In opposition to simple universes, we can define a *complex structure* linking two or more universes in a single structure so that there is a detailed correspondence between the components. A complex structure formed by two components can be called a *dual structure*. Based on Evans' elaboration of Walton's theory, we can analyze the mud-pie game as a tiny dual structure made up of two small universes linked by the relation of correspondence "will be taken as." In the *Magnum Opus* describing the first universe we will find, say, the inventory of beings belonging to it: Mary, Peter, Karen, globs of mud, small black pebbles, a metal object, followed by a description of the children manipulating the mud and pebbles. The *Magnum Opus* of the second universe will list three cooks, pies, raisins, a hot oven, and describe the skillful preparation of the raisin pies. A book that can be called the *Book of Correspondence* will spell out the relation "will be taken as" that consists precisely of Evans' basic principles: it will specify that Mary in the first universe shall be taken as a cook in the second universe, that globs of mud in the first universe shall be taken as pies in the second universe, and so on.

## Salient Structures: Religious and Fictional

Since the really real world enjoys a definite ontological priority over the world of make-believe, we may distinguish between primary and secondary universes within dual structures, the former constituting the foundation upon which the latter is built. In our example, the world of the children playing in the mud functions as the primary universe, while the world of cooks and pies is assigned the place of secondary universe. As we saw, the two universes are linked by a relation of correspondence, which in our example yields an isomorphism, since to every element in the primary universe the relation "will be taken as" assigns one and only one element in the secondary universe. To use a term introduced by Evans, one can characterize such a situation as an *existentially conservative* dual structure: no element in the secondary world of make-believe lacks a correspondent in the primary universe. There are, however, games of make-believe in which entities exist that have no correspondent in the real world. Calling these games *existentially creative,* Evans brings as examples shadow boxing, in which one pretends to fight an opponent, or the game of pretending to be followed by a dragon.

I shall call *salient* structures those dual structures in which the primary universe does not enter into an isomorphism with the secondary universe, because the latter includes entities and states of affairs that lack a correspondent in the former. (The converse may also be true, but it is not required by the definition.) Such structures are not restricted to games of make-believe. They have long been used by the religious mind as a fundamental ontological model. As shown by the analyses of Max Weber, Rudolf Otto, Roger Caillois, Mircea Eliade, and Peter Berger, the religious mind divides the universe into two regions qualitatively different: space is partitioned into sacred regions, endowed with reality in the strongest sense, and nonsacred places that lack consistency; sacred cyclical time diverges from profane time and its irreversible duration. According to Eliade, "the religious experience of the non-homogeneity of space is a primordial experience, homologizable to a founding of the world."[10] When stating that he is at the Center of the World, the Kwakiutl neophyte does not deny his presence in the cult hut next to the sacred pole; he rather asserts a doubly articulated ontology in which one level rests upon the other. An ontological model containing two frames of reference that are as distinct as possible, though closely related, represents religious consciousness.

And it can be argued that when Arthur Danto describes the ontology of artworks, he employs a salient model: scrutinizing the uses of *is* in relation to works of art he notices that it is equally true to assert that "This actor *is* Lear" and "This actor *is not* Lear." The first use he calls the *is of artistic identification* and remarks that "It is an *is*, incidentally, which has near-relatives in marginal and mythical pronouncements. (Thus, one *is* Quetzalcoatl; those *are* the Pillars of Hercules.)" And also: "the artworld stands to the real world in something like the relationship in which the City of God stands to the Earthly City" (1964, pp. 137, 139). In *The Transfiguration of the Commonplace* Danto develops the distinction between the artwork and its material support, claiming that the distinction is ontological; and indeed, since the ontology of the work cannot be reduced to that of its material, the relationship is salient in the above sense. Joseph Margolis (1977) calls the pattern *emergence* and assumes that it constitutes a crucial ontological trait of artistic works.

Sometimes literary texts explicitly thematize a dual structure: in Borges' "The Library of Babel,"

> The universe (which others call the Library) is composed of an indefinite, perhaps an infinite, number of hexagonal galleries, with enormous ventilation shafts in the middle, encircled by very low railings. From any hexagon, the upper and lower stories are visible, interminably.

Positing a universe organized differently from the one we happen to inhabit, Borges' text sketches a detailed secondary ontology containing objects, properties, relations. We understand the secondary ontology by virtue of the primary: "galleries," "ventilation shafts," "railings," "hexagonal," "low," which are terms transported, as it were, from the nonfictional universe. In a gesture of politeness, we are also offered the key to the relation between the two ontologies: the secondary one is modeled as a library, which of course does not mean that the new universe should be understood as belonging to the class of objects called "libraries" in the primary ontology, since the term does not designate any of the libraries of the actual world. If we grasp its significance, however, it is because we know what kind of object the libraries-in-the-actual-world are, and we feel free to relate the library-in-the-story-by-Borges to these. In the same way, we are prepared to relate each object in the story to some object in our world, by virtue of the relations of correspondence, whose role is to ensure the correct grasping of the structure of the secondary ontology as both different from and based upon the primary ontology.

Discourse-oriented analysis of fiction claims that fictional terms only mean but do not denote in the actual world and that, in Searle's formula, "in *Little Red Riding Hood* both . . . 'red' means red and yet . . . the rules correlating 'red' with red are not in force" (1975b, p. 319). What happens in fact is that the rules correlating "red"-in-the-second-ontology with red-in-the-first-ontology are more complex than the rules relating "red" with red in the first ontology, and since the first ontology serves as the ontic foundation of the fictional ontology, "red"-in-fiction is matched with red-in-the-really-real-world only indirectly, via the correspondence relations. From the way we define these relations, it is clear that nothing forces us to relate the two kinds of red: the writer of fiction can always fabricate a story about a land where red is in fact green. Or he can devise a secondary ontology in which agents shaped as human beings correspond to abstract qualities in the primary ontology. A character named Death advances on stage and recites:

> Lo, yonder I see Everyman walking.
> Full little he thinketh on my coming;
> His mind is on fleshly lusts and his treasure,
> And great pain it shall cause him to endure
> Before the Lord, heaven King.
>
> *[Enter Everyman]*
>
> Everyman, stand still? Whither are thou going
> Thus gaily? Hast thou thy Maker forget?

Here the spectator sees a well-individuated entity carrying attributes that in the primary world relate to an event (death) and not to an individual. Allegory uses relations of correspondence less straightforward than realist novels, but even the latter's links to the primary world are highly mediated. Even if Mr. Pickwick's absence from Oxford, or his generosity or lack of tact, resemble actual Englishmen's properties more than Everyman's or Death's actions do, we construe *The Pickwick Papers* precisely by establishing links between the secondary world and the primary through an intellectual operation similar to the understanding of allegory. When Paul de Man (1983) argued that allegory is the central topos of literature, he based his demonstration on semiotic and phenomenological arguments, and identified allegory with the movement of temporality. The logic of fictional worlds vindicates his results, by suggesting that allegorical reading provides for the most general pattern of decoding relations or correspondence within fictional structures. That allegory proper—the use of fairly complex correspondence—is only seldom put to use in fiction must be attributed to convenience: in order to be manageable, secondary ontologies have to respect as much as possible the inner structure of the primary ontologies they use as their foundation. In a sense, this is a problem of artistic economy; as F. E. Sparshott noticed, in the extreme cases of science fiction "either the place and the participants are conceived on the model of familiar types, in which case the element of fantasy becomes scarcely more than decoration, or the story becomes thin and schematic, because we cannot tell what sort of background to provide for what we are explicitly told" (1967, p. 5).

If sacred and fictional worlds share the two-level organization and the allegorical links between the primary and the secondary ontologies, my example of the mime can be better explained: the actor's body and movements, as they exist in the actual world, serve as a primary universe, as a foundation for the secondary universe in which the mime becomes the saintly priest blessing the crowd. But was his blessing effective? In other words, did the secondary universe genuinely return and interact with the primary universe? If the answer is yes, if the mime, beyond *mimicking* the sacred *enacted* it, if beyond mere representation of the divine he made it present, then the performance transcended fiction, in spite of the usual conventions and conditions of felicity. Since cult and fiction differ merely in the strength of the secondary universe, when sufficient energy is channeled into mimetic acts, these may leave the fictional mode and cross the threshold of actuality. The myth of Pygmalion narrates this transformation. And perhaps here lies the reason why fictional and sacred worlds, ready as they are for unexpected mutations, need a differentiation of the notion of being. In the ontology of the sacred, the plenary reality of the sacred domain is crucially opposed to the precarious existence of the profane. Sacred beings not only obey different laws than do sublunar creatures, but their way of being is fundamentally different (to use Rudolf Otto's well-known formula). Theology, which has reflected at length on this aspect of sacred universes, has arrived at the theory of the analogy of being, according to which the verb *to be* is only analogically asserted of God and his creatures.[11]

This type of predication should be extended to fictional constructions; it can be argued that, in fiction, being is only analogically similar to the same notion in plain ontologies. But while sacred worlds overflow with energy, fictional activities represent a weaker form of dual structure. The loss of energy prevents fictional games from leaping into actuality: effective grace is replaced with catharsis, revelation with interpretation, ecstasy with playfulness. As a game of make-believe, fiction obeys rules and conventions; whereas belief in the myths of the community is compulsory, assent to fiction is free and clearly circumscribed in time and space. Myths, moreover, are all supposedly fixed in advance and true forever, but new fictional constructions, like new games, remain always possible.

## Salient Structures: Their Representation in Fiction

As metaphysical models, salient structures enjoy considerable generality, going beyond the various literary and aesthetic purposes pursued by individual texts. Yet these notions can also serve as analytical tools, especially in relation to the inner structure of literary universes.[12] *Don Quixote,* for instance, has a complex world structure, the components of which do not always logically harmonize with one another. Leaving aside some of the less central stylistic effects such as the question of the main narrator (who is he? Cervantes? Cid Hamet?), the events of the novel take place in two parallel sets of worlds. One set has as its actual world the characters and the events given as real in the novel: the infatuation of a certain Alonso Quixana with chivalric stories, his first escape, his adventures. A number of possible worlds are linked to the actual-in-the-novel world by the usual relation of alternativeness. Such is, for instance, the world in which the priest, the barber, the other of Quixana's friends manage to prevent him from escaping a second time. The second set of worlds is existentially creative, in Evans' sense; it blends the world actual in the novel and the worlds given as actual in the romances devoutly believed by Quixote. The individuals who populate Quixote's world are characters of the novel written by Cervantes mixed with characters of the chivalric stories. Again, besides the basic Quixotic, there are many possible alternate Quixotic worlds, such as the world in which Quixote succeeds in defeating the giants disguised as windmills. One of the main aesthetic effects of the novel is the ambiguity of raw events:

any such event can be incorporated into the set of worlds actual in the novel, and into the set of Quixotic worlds as well. Sancho Panza's puzzle originates precisely in his inability to adhere firmly to one of these sets of worlds: his willingness to share Quixote's worlds is constantly hampered by the more natural interpretation of what happens in terms of the worlds actual and possible in the novel.

A more modern example of this technique is offered by T. H. White's *The Once and Future King*. This novel is simultaneously set in medieval times at King Arthur's court and in late nineteenth- and early twentieth-century imperial Great Britain. The set of worlds actual and possible in the novel thus resemble to some extent Quixote's worlds: there is a continuous hesitation between two frames of reference. However, while in Cervantes' text Quixote is the only character who simultaneously lives in the two frames of reference, in White's novel the entire text oscillates between medieval and modern times; and if in *Don Quixote* the world in the novel serves as a firm background against which the hero's delusion can be measured and defused, White writes about a world structure in which no frame of reference prevails. In such cases, and in many others, the notion of *world of the work of art* refers to a complex entity that needs careful logical and aesthetic disentangling: the worlds that mix together in texts may resemble the actual world, but they may be impossible or erratic worlds as well. Works of fiction more or less dramatically combine incompatible world-structures, play with the impossible, and incessantly speak about the unspeakable. Yet they most often present themselves as linguistically coherent texts, gently obeying stylistic and generic conventions, and it is no small feat that we manage to put together heteregeneous sets of fictional worlds in unified, beautifully varnished texts, and to make sense of the tension between texts and worlds.

As we have seen earlier, fiction, like sacred worlds, is based on salient structures. The mime's body serves as a primary layer on which is built the secondary universe of the priest and his blessings; he who in our world is only an actor *is* Lear in the secondary world of the performance; Paris, the real city, is also the recondite location of Eugene Sue's novels or the place swarming with the strong, idiosyncratic characters of Balzac's *Scènes de la vie parisienne* or else the monotonous, agitated city of Flaubert's *L'Education sentimentale*. Yet the salient ontology of fiction, as a general model, is not necessarily thematized as such by all literary texts. The universe described in Beckett's *Molloy* appears to be made up of a single ontological layer:

I am in my mother's room. It's I who live there now. I don't know
how I got there. Perhaps in an ambulance, certainly a vehicle of some
kind. I was helped. I'd never have got there alone. There's a man
who comes every week. Perhaps I got there thanks to him. He says
not.

In spite of its simplicity, the one-layer universe is only imperfectly
mastered by the narrator, who often is at a loss in identifying beings
or attributing qualities to them: Molloy shares the shyness of many
contemporary narrators who, overwhelmed by the universes they
inhabit, do not dare confront them other than locally and only with
utmost caution. In contrast, medieval passion plays confidently handle
huge universes, split into a sacred and a profane level, in constant
interaction. That the meaning of heroic prose, of most Greek tragedies, of some Renaissance dramas, of many contemporary poems,
would be unintelligible without reference to dual structures does not,
however, entail that ontological complexity in fiction must be limited
to the representation of the sacred-profane duality. As the examples
of *Don Quixote* and *The Once and Future King* show, such complexity
can originate in one character's idiosyncratic organization of the universe, as opposed to the actuality-in-the-novel; or else in the vacillation of the narrative base itself between two different "actualities."
In such texts the mere representation of a nonproblematic salient
structure, as it occurs in medieval texts, gives way to a thematization
of ontological complexities. Juggling with ontological structures in
fiction is a widespread device in late Renaissance and Baroque literature, signaled by the frequent occurrence of the play-inside-the-play
(*The Spanish Tragedy, Hamlet, The Taming of the Shrew*). Fictitious
ontologies are limpidly schematized in the first part of *Quixote,* in
which the hero embraces a frame of interpretation fit only for medieval romance and applies it to the actual world of the novel. In the
second part, the situation becomes more intricate, with Quixote
showing a diminishing commitment to his earlier frame of interpretation, but without plainly abjuring it before the end of the text. This
poses the delicate problem of *gradual* adhesion to an internal model
or another, perhaps even of the gradual validity of such model. To
diversify the picture even more, the fictional hero Quixote, who in
the basic world of the novel is as actual as can be, reads Avellaneda's
unauthorized continuation of Cervante's first part and learns there
about the unauthentic Quixote, who is fictional with respect to the
world of the "real" Quixote. The "real" hidalgo then proceeds to

demonstrate the falsity of Avellaneda's account, which he victoriously refutes by mere comparison with the "real" facts, found in Cervantes' account. In the ontology *in* fiction inhabited by Quixote, he examines an ontology *of* fiction, by comparing Avellaneda's world to his own.[13] Delightfully deceptive, such a baroque vortex vividly thematizes the predicament of fictional space: texts always flirt with the self-referential temptation and the intoxicating games of higher-order fictionality. But the uneasy relations between worlds and texts have deeper semantic roots.

## From Worlds to Texts: Intricacies and Legends

According to the definition proposed earlier, a universe is composed of a base—an actual world—surrounded by a constellation of alternative worlds. In Plantinga's view, an unproblematic correspondence relates each of these worlds to a book assumed to contain all true sentences about the world. I labeled *Magnum Opus* the set of books about the universe written in some language *L*. The *Magnum Opus* contains, in addition to every book about the worlds, a *Book of Rules* that includes higher-order considerations about the universe, its worlds, and the language of the *Magnum Opus*. The Quinean principle of indeterminacy, generalized by Putnam to possible-world systems, has, however, the consequence that to each world of a universe will correspond a considerable, perhaps even an infinite, number of books; hence the number of *Magna Opera* associated with a universe will be of an even greater magnitude. Let us call the set of all *Magna Opera* about a universe the Total Image of that universe. Since there are insuperable problems with infinite sets of sentences, especially when the order of infinity goes beyond the continuum threshold (which should be the case if, for instance, the universe included all transfinite numbers), I should hasten to add that I do not have the slightest idea as to what such a Total Image would look like. Moise Cordovero's *Torah* contained 340,000 apparent letters and 600,000 mysterious letters, one for each individual belonging to Israel. Innumerable as it might have once seemed, this book, like Borges' "Library of Babel," is only a miniaturized version of the Total Image. Besides its inconceivable magnitude, and the purely quantitative problems this poses for any conceivable language, the universe might happen to be radically indescribable. Therefore only an infinite, omniscient God, as described by medieval theology, could master, in an entirely mysterious way, the Total Image of the universe.

The very inscrutability of the Total Image helps us to grasp what it would really mean to *fully describe* a universe, and how far away from any imaginable linguistic experience this notion is. A text thus can only be an infinitesimally partial description of its universe—even to arrive at its minuscule level, complex processing is necessary.

Through what principles such processing would work is impossible to ascertain. A half-forgotten legend tells us, however, that among the innumerable books about various universes, each cut to astronomical size, there exists a series of volumes modest in their object, language and theory that handle states of affairs of our actual world in a human language and in terms of common sense. They are called the Daily Books. Of these books, humans only know tiny fragments, since no one but a supernatural being could master them in their entirety. Indeed, the custody of the Eternal Books has been entrusted to benevolent genies, distantly related to Laplace's omniscient and inoffensive demon. Moreover, it is said, each of us has been assigned to one of these spirits, on the day of our birth. According to some, these custodians are there to supervise our behavior and every day mark a purple tick before every proposition in the *Magnum Opus* made true by our deeds and projects, beliefs and certitudes, feelings and desires, and every night include them in a Daily Book that will be used on the Day of Judgment. Others say that they do not just passively record the sentences of the *Magna Opera* that our life renders actual but actively write down our destiny, by preparing in advance the Daily Books we obediently follow. In either case, the Daily Books include sentences from various books of the *Magnum Opus,* some belonging to the description of the actual world, some to that of its possible alternatives (since desires, projects, and beliefs require reference to possible worlds). A Daily Book will then be a set of sentences representing the destiny of a single individual during a single day. It possesses a *refraction index* that indicates the angle under which it has been cut from the *Magnum Opus.*

But the Higher Authority for which our custodian works does not have enough time or patience to read the entire Daily Book. To please it, in addition to writing these records, the nimble custodian must sort and rearrange the sets of sentences. He is, for instance, expected to narrate the life of his client; this means that after listing the true sentences, he must order some of them in temporal sequence, eliminate others, indicate principles of causality and purposefulness, perhaps add certain evaluating statements in the light of the norms respected in that part of the universe. In short, he must construct a system, propose a theory.

Some add that he is required to shorten the innumerable pages of the Daily Books as well and write more compact accounts: yearbooks or, even better, a single book on the entire life of his subject. The causal connections between sentences, the range of purposes, must reach a wider scope; the norms are applied to a larger number of actions. Consequently the generalizations look bolder, and the theory underlying the Lifebook is endowed with a richer content. The refraction index narrows down further, so as to include not only a selection of sentences but also an organization of these into a relevant account. And since the Judgment purports to be a fair one and the hero of the Lifebook is allowed to defend himself, his only recourse will be to challenge the system and not the sentences, since these are unmistakably true. The defendant almost always chooses to present an alternate Lifebook or fragment thereof, with a slightly different refraction index, in which a different interpretation makes use of the same set of sentences. If, for instance, he were to ask for a change in the weight assigned to each sentence, a single good deed could atone for scores of sins.

It must be noted, in addition, that the Eternal Judge does not examine only our moral destiny but also controls all movement in his universe, and as a consequence the spirits that have access to the Eternal Books do not only write reports on individual destinies but supervise and record more complex situations as well: histories of entire groups of people united by their family links, tribes, nations; handbooks of celestial movement; musical treatises. Each such book displays a refraction index—a selection of sentences—and a theory that organizes them into a readable book. In his infinite fairness, the Judge may require several spirits to report on the same question; accordingly, the books produced may well differ from one another, since each genie may select another set of sentences and organize them differently. Some will accuse, some will ask forgiveness, still others will profess indifference.

It has also long been noticed that if the Daily Books are to be thoroughly prepared, and the Yearbooks, Lifebooks, Family Books, and Books of Nations likewise, they cannot be limited to a single underlying theory or to a single language. In some cases Daily Books may have to contain descriptions of states of affairs that require more than one theory: some complicated individuals need Daily Books listing notions of Keplerian astronomy, along with a more archaic, biblical cosmology, reflecting their various beliefs. Since each *Magnum Opus* has its own theoretical bias, the nimble genie will achieve his task by compiling sentences from the *Magna Opera* based on the biblical theory and from those sensitive to more recent astronomy. It is impossible to limit the genie to a single *Magnum Opus* obeying common sense: his task forces him to jump from one infinitely large set of books to another, selecting sentences and mixing them together according to an *aggregation recipe* that indicates the requested proportions of fragments to be derived from different *Magna Opera*.

This is all the more necessary when the genie prepares the account of a nation's life or a family's history: the aggregation recipe will then have to include material from highly incompatible *Magna Opera,* mixing contradictory projects, incoherent desires, and polemic images of the world. A careful metatextual notation helps some of the tidiest genies to keep their books in order; those who choose to employ it attach to every sentence a sign of origin to remind themselves whence they copied it. Moreover, they can separate contradictory chunks of their work by carefully indicating whose beliefs or desires are handled in every instance. As a result, their writings will be heterogeneous books, made up of various fragments of *Magna Opera,* mixing languages and theories, refracting them according to precise backgrounds and needs.

In spite of this metatextual notation, a modern logician considering such books would no doubt be horrified by their inconsistency and incompleteness. But the picture sometimes gets even worse. Some of the genies in charge of the preparation of the books are not as gentle and skillful as others. They may be quite mischievous spirits, not very deft with the books, who do not limit themselves to those opera based on good theories and displaying some form of imprimatur, but often go rummaging in the wrong *Magna Opera,* based on theories false or condemned. Or perhaps there is no way of knowing for certain which *Magna Opera* are truthful and which are not. In particular, one clumsy genie is known to mix sentences on the actual world and sentences on its alternatives, such that the final outcome of his activity is not only scattered with false sentences but also presents as actual sentences those true only in possible worlds and, as merely possible, sentences true in the actual world. And as if these transgressions were not enough, the mischievous genie takes secret strolls to the forbidden section of the infinite library, called *Impossi-*

*bilia*. About the folios hidden there not much is known, but the effect of the genie's visits is often reflected in the composition of the books he prepares, books that are incongruously replete with sentences impossible in the actual world and in its alternatives. Moreover, out of carelessness or ill intention or both, our genie does not use metatextual notation to help his reader trace down the origin of various parts of his book; consequently, detecting the sentences originating in the *Impossibilia* or separating the possible states of affairs from the actual ones becomes an exceedingly difficult task.

Other spirits, more careful in their undertakings, complain to the Judge and, denouncing the genie who uses the forbidden *Impossibilia,* claim that his unreliable books threaten the entire system of Eternal records. Should the Judge punish him? Should the dark side of the library be more effectively secluded? Summoned to speak in his own defense, the careless genie points out that his respected brothers take liberties with the *Magna Opera* too; that every selection, every mixing of sentences from various opera involves interpretations of the Eternal Books. Humans judged according to the righteous accounts often feel wronged and lodge appeals, pointing to various forgotten sentences; sometimes they obtain a change in judgment. Stars and planets complain about the mathematical descriptions and often cause a change in the books about their movements. Our genie, on the other hand, seldom offends inhabitants of the cosmos: were there ever complaints against his rummaging through the *Impossibilia?* When his human clients are judged, do they rebel against his procedure? Those who find their books enriched with impossible events and beings usually rejoice, since humans love to dream; as for those whose Eternal destiny is threatened by such extensions of their books, they can always disclaim them as fictitious. And how can *Impossibilia* be eradicated? Are they not spontaneously generated by the strength of any language? Does not every idiom project innumerable *Impossibilia?* And do the righteous spirits know that the dark side of the library is full of movement, just like its bright side? That with each new Daily Book, Yearbook, or Book of the Planets and Stars, new multitudes of *Impossibilia* are born, for many impossible books are but impossible-in-the-light-of-a-given-possible-book? Did they know that some of the folios in the *Impossibilia* are identical with some authorized books, that among books written by humans one often finds impossible sentences, that in the most innocuous Daily Account allusions to such *Impossibilia* can be found, and that all spirits who prepared Daily or Year Books must have inserted impossible sentences in their texts, for the mixture between *Possibilia* and *Impossibilia* is inextricable. Our books, he would add, are all *Miscellanea,* governed by refraction indexes and aggregation recipes! Their relation to the *Magna Opera* is tortuous and unpredictable; heteronomy sets apart books and worlds.

But the Eternal Judge keeps silent, allowing the righteous genies to expel the wrongdoer. Filled with sadness, he takes refuge on earth, in the hope that humans will treat him better. Alas, during countless adventures, worth the pen of a Borgesian Hašek, he will gradually discover that earthly books are even less coherent than heavenly Miscellanea, since humans do not possess the strength of vision or the agility of spirits. Human books, imperfect imitations, contain but tiny fragments of *Miscellanea,* collected in *Compendia* fit for finite intellects. Some of these *Compendia,* not even couched in writing, survive as oral products: myths and poems of legendary heroes, and also rules that govern social life are kept in unwritten *Compendia* and transmitted from mouth to mouth by oral initiation. Oral and written compendia cannot include all the contents of the miscellany they imitate, as our fallen genie soon discovers; he may therefore assume that each compendium is put together according to a *selection principle,* retaining only parts of the miscellany in accordance with various practices and needs. He can read the narrative compendia on the lives and deeds of famous Greek and Roman men and silently wonder about the numerous aspects present in the heavenly Miscellanies on the same subject, but left aside in the earthly texts. Later he can browse through other narrative compendia on the same topic, in the hope that they would come close to the model and neglect less the essentials of the correspondent miscellany. Soon he will understand that no one-to-one correspondence of compendia to miscellanies ever occurs. Oral and written compendia are subject to later revision, changes, degradation, contamination. And well before reaching that stage, at the very moment of their conception, compendia often derive from more than one miscellany. Astonished by human ignorance of the hereafter, the genie might read the New Testament, which he would perceive as an attempt to integrate the Jewish Bible and new miscellanies; the Koran in which he would detect echoes from the two Testaments; Mani's writings and their attempt to encompass all the compendia of contemporary religions. If miscellanies mix together sentences belonging to various *Magna Opera* according to an aggregation recipe, compendia amalgamate fragmentary contents of several miscellanies.

But, as the genie would soon discover, while miscellanies, destined for eternal minds, have no need of stylistic artifices, compendia, whose readers belong to the whimsical, inattentive and forgetful human species, are subject to *structural constraints:* they are often couched in an especially rich and memorable language and organize the contents in a highly rhetorical way. When such constraints are present, humans call the compendium a *text.* But since structural constraints claim a certain independence of operation, and a text can be put together by combining fragments of different compendia, heteronomy strikes again and blurs the purity of correspondence between the texts and compendia.

In the end, humans can understand the fallen genie even less than can his former fellow angels. But his journey has not been in vain; if earlier he had understood that heteronomy mars the correspondence between worlds and heavenly books, he can now accept that the long chain of imperfect agreements continues throughout the sublunar realm. Worlds are separated from human texts by a long chain of intermediaries: *Magna Opera,* which are inconceivably infinite collections of books couched in a given language, are processed into miscellanies, vast selections of sentences from various *Magna Opera,* accumulated for a certain purpose, covering a certain domain, and expressing a more or less coherent theory. Through a renewed process of selection, miscellanea are cut down to compendia, which, once structurally organized, become texts. To his heavenly ears, human talk about the world of a text would sound merely as an abridged way of referring to the complex links between structured texts, their unstructured propositional content (the compendium), the quite heterogeneous world views on which they are based (the miscellanies), and finally the complete descriptions in the books of the *Magna Opera.* At each step of this gnostic procession a principle of noncoincidence is at work: the myriads of books swarming in the *Magna Opera* are improperly combined in miscellanies; in turn compendia link together fragments of miscellanies, letting their strong individuality fade away; last but not least, texts reorganize compendia according to their own autonomous needs. Deeply embedded in texts, heterogeneity prevents any clearcut correspondence between the levels of procession. Choosing in his affliction to forget language, the fallen genie will undergo a long and lonely initiation to eternal silence.

## The Threefold Nature of Fictionality

The above story, its sad conclusion notwithstanding, suggests a geological view of texts: like bedrock, texts amalgamate strata of diverse geological origins. Pressed together by the cohesive forces of petrifaction, the color and texture of these strata refer back to their birthplace; it is the task of enlightened analysis to reflect not only on various structural constraints and on textual coherence, but also on the deeply ingrained semantic heteronomy of texts, on the principle of dispersion embedded in them.

The question of fiction itself undergoes a considerable change. For, if texts are not uniformly related to books on worlds, if at each step heteronomy and dislocation intervene to blur the picture, there is no guarantee that all sentences of the text can be traced back to one and the same world, or to the same universe. But since the number of universes is indefinitely large, and since some universes are incompatible with others, mixing fragments from various lines of actuality and possibility leads to miscellanies and texts more or less divergent from one another, to the point that some texts, collecting their substance from far away universes, from impossible worlds, from discarded magna opera, may cross a certain threshold and be readier than others for a fictional reading. The dual ontology of fiction reflects, in a simplified way, the deep heterogeneity of texts. But since mixture and not homogeneity governs textual matters, fiction does not constitute the exception one is tempted to believe. Its semantic duality merely intensifies a more general feature of texts, thus revealing under a particularly clear light the more general heteronomy of texts.

Moreover, the fictionality of a text is not always grounded in its semantic composition. If a text speaks about impossible objects (the Aleph) it will certainly be understood as fictitious on semantic grounds: the universe where alephs exist lies far away from ours, in the fictional direction, and the *Magnum Opus* in which sentences about it originate must be kept with the least accessible *Impossibilia*. But miscellanies and compendia, once constituted, can *become* fictive, by a change of attitude toward their validity; the belated fictionality of aging myths has pragmatic causes. At the level of texts, too, cultural traditions ossify certain kinds of structural constraints for fiction, with the result that texts which are nonfictional on semantic or pragmatic grounds can be read fictionally for purely textual reasons: well-written memoirs or romanced biographies are obvious examples.

The theory of fiction is therefore faced with three intimately connected areas of inquiry: semantic aspects, which in addition to metaphysical questions include demarcational problems such as the borders of fiction, the distance between fictional and nonfictional universes, the size and structure of the former; the pragmatics of fiction, which may be expected to examine fiction as an institution and its place within culture; and the stylistic and textual constraints related to fictional genres and conventions.

# 4 ～ Border, Distance, Size, Incompleteness

THE PICTURE sketched in the last chapter suggests a most complex and unstable relationship between texts and worlds, with various levels of heterogeneity preventing texts from faithfully depicting worlds.[1] Construed as linguistic conformity between worlds and their texts, realism is a remarkably courageous project. Even to speak of "their" texts with respect to worlds is an act of faith, since the indeterminacy of reference and the labyrinth of universes seem to preclude such firm attachments. Yet indeterminacy is compensated for by the strength of our ontological commitments. We confidently regard our worlds as unified and coherent; we also treat them as economical collections of beings, our fits of ontological prodigality notwithstanding. Since coherence and economy may not stand up to scrutiny, we most often start by refraining from close examination. The worlds we speak about, actual or fictional, neatly hide their deep fractures, and our language, our texts, appear for a while to be transparent media unproblematically leading to worlds. For, before confronting higher-order perplexities, we explore the realms described by compendia and texts, which stimulate our sense of referential adventure and, in a sense, serve as mere paths of access to worlds: once the goal is reached, the events of the journey may be forgotten.

To such forgetfulness, the New Critics' insistence on close reading ironically stands witness, since it aims at forcing us to become aware of the subtleties and meanderings of texts: the very need for deliberate calling of attention to the pleasures of the journey is an indicator of how little inclined we are to enjoy them, naturally hurried as we are toward the worlds themselves. Our memory seems mostly to register facts and characters, an even when we do remember isolated lines, we usually select gnomic and aphoristic passages, as if an irrepressible referential instinct presses us to go beyond the textual medium. Text transcending serves us well, especially when worlds belonging to the same family are reached through both textual and nontextual means. *Romans á clef* are so delightful precisely because, by guiding us to the same territories as extratextual knowledge, they bestow a sense of fulfillment upon our textual adventures. The same is true of book illustrations: looking at the etchings of Gustave Doré for Rabelais's *Gargantua,* we recognize the figure of the giant hero not by virtue of particular textual artifices but because we have processed the textual information, leaving aside most stylistic and narratological effects.

Yet it would seem that knowledge of worlds is strictly dependent on their manifestation, textual or otherwise. The only way of learning about *Hamlet,* most critics would assert, is by studying its text. Texts, media, are not just referential paths leading to worlds: to read a text or to look at a painting means already to inhabit their worlds. To argue that we easily forget textual beauties while we remember facts and events derives from a natural propensity to register essential elements and to disregard circumstantial information; but such a propensity does not necessarily entail that we first read texts, then reach the worlds and discard the medium. And visiting worlds, not unlike visiting people or places, can have various purposes, such as deriving information, benefit, or pleasure. We sometimes vaguely reconnoiter a new territory; on other occasions we proceed straight to the re-examination of a well-known detail. Reading a text in order to learn how to orient ourselves in the world depicted by it is not the same endeavor as assenting to a world in order to explore and enjoy a text. Formalist aesthetics and poetics claimed that in literature the powers of attention focus on the medium rather than on reference. The poetic function shifts our interest to the message as an aim in itself; reference loses its autonomy and integrates itself into the poetic compactness of the message. But perhaps this does not happen only to poetic texts and aesthetic objects; a widespread philosophical position denies referential effectiveness even to nonpoetic worlds. Various neo-Kantian approaches assume that there are no worlds strictly speaking, but only world-versions occasioned by theories, texts, works of art, with no autonomous existence outside these. To the referential paradigm that, unduly perhaps, generalizes realist schemata to fictional activity, we find here a counterpart wherein poetic intimacy between a text and a idiosyncratic world is generalized to all types of knowledge.

For such perplexities there is no ready solution in sight, since more often than not plainly referential views are assumed to be too unsophisticated for aesthetic objects: is not strong realism often tempted to dismiss fiction as false or spurious discourse? To accept that fictional texts can provide a privileged path of access to the world, on the other hand, may foster relativism. The example of Nelson Goodman, who restored literary and artistic fiction to a position of legitimacy within the framework of analytical philosophy, is significant. Read metaphorically, fictional texts are promoted by Goodman to a world-version status equivalent to the results of physics; but this does not entail that a verion is "right" (the term "true" is avoided) when it applies to its world: "we might better say that 'the world' depends on its rightness." We do not judge a version as "right" by relating it to its world; rather, "all we learn about the world is contained in right versions of it, and while the underlying world, bereft of these, need not be denied to those who lose it, it is perhaps on the whole a world well lost" (1978, p. 4). Thus there are no independent means of discovering whether a version is "right" or not other than obedience to the various versions or some "rightness" instinct. The desire not do dismiss the medium leads, for all practical purposes, to the loss of the worlds.

But would this not, again, lead to the neglect of what internal models can show us—the detailed meanderings and obstacles of our journeys through fictional spaces?

## Borders of Fiction: Mythification and Fictional Expansion

We saw earlier how various types of segregationism answer the demarcational question by positing clearcut limits between the actual world and the worlds of fiction. Often the decision has metaphysical grounds: since actual worlds appear to be undoubtedly real, complete, and consistent, while fictional worlds are intrinsically incomplete and inconsistent, the latter are best seen as inconsequential constructions of our mind. Incomplete—how many children did Lady Macbeth have? This question is impossible to answer, since no progress of science would ever clarify the situation. Inconsistent—both sentences are true.

(1)  Sherlock Holmes lived on Baker Street.

(2)  Sherlock Holmes did not live on Baker Street.

Helplessly imaginary—no one in need of a private detective would seek Sherlock Holmes's help. But are not incompleteness, inconsistency, unreality the least commendable qualities of worlds? Should not fictional territories be surrounded by a sanitary borderline?

Yet a segregationist decision, plausible as it may be at the metaphorical level, does not necessarily reflect cultural practices at the institutional level. Most contemporary readers are indeed institutionally aware of the difference between fact and fiction, but this is by no means the universal pattern. To use a geographic simile, the fact that the contemporary world has been carefully divided into territories does not mean that our institution of well-defined international boundaries has always been in place. Even today, border crossing can take various forms; some borders are mutually permeable (United States and Canada), others are highly selective (Russia and China) or asymmetric (Austria and Czechoslovakia), or even impenetrable (Israel and Syria). These examples involve differences of mutual accessibility; in all the examples the boundaries are nevertheless well-defined, stable lines between states, the countours of which are a matter of public knowledge. But consider societies without sharp boundaries: village groups confined to the clearings of the primitive forest, pastoral societies autonomous and without borders, the North African nomads, or the great dromocracies, the maritime empires under Japan or Great Britain, built along trade arteries. More rigid boundaries appeared relatively late: Sebastian Münster's *Cosmographia* (1544) still proposes linguistic borders between European kingdoms, and the first reliable map of France was not drawn before the end of the eighteenth century. In 1789, the year of the French Revolution, it was still impossible to determine the limits of France, in the modern sense of the term. And yet, according to eighteenth-century standards, France was a disciplined and unified territory. The modern concept of rigid boundary gradually developed only after the Napoleonic wars and culminated with the redrawing of the European map after the First World War.[2]

In a similar fashion, the strict delimitation of boundaries between fictional and nonfictional territories is not a universal phenomenon. Fictional domains have undergone a long process of structuring, ossification, and delimitation. It is commonplace to remark that most often archaic epic and dramatic literary artifacts do not have fictive settings, at least for their primary users. The characters of these were heroes and gods, beings endowed with as much reality as myth can provide. For, in the eyes of its users, a myth exemplifies the very paradigm of truth: Zeus, Hercules, Pallas Athena, Aphrodite, Agamemnon, Paris, Helen, Iphigenia, and Oedipus were not fictional in any sense of the term. Not that they were felt as simply belonging to the same level of reality as common mortals. As we saw earlier, the universe of societies that believe in myths unfolds at two different levels: the profane reality, characterized by ontological paucity and precariousness, contrasts with a mythical level, ontologically self-sufficient, containing a privileged space and a cyclical time. Gods and heroes inhabit the sacred space, but this space is not felt fictional: if anything, it is endowed with *more* weight and stability than the mortals' spaces. Eliade, who has written some of the most vivid descriptions of the sacred ontologies of archaic cultures, relates an amusing story that shows how an everyday happening becomes a mythical story (1955, pp. 19–20).

A Romanian folklorist doing field work in Maramuresh finds a heretofore unknown ballad. It tells the story of a young bridegroom bewitched by a jealous mountain fairy who, a few days before the young man's marriage, pushes him off a precipice; next day a group of shepherds find the body and bring it back to the village, where the bride meets them and sings a beautiful funeral lamentation. Inquiring about the date of the event, the researcher is told that it happened long ago, *in illo tempore*. Pressing the question, he learns that the events go back only forty years and that the bride is still alive. He visits her and hears her own version of the story: the victim of a banal accident, her fiancé fell into a crevice but did not die on the spot; his cries for help were heard by a few neighbors who transported him to the village, where he passed away soon after. When the folklorist returns to the village with the authentic story, pointing out that there was no jealous mountain fairy involved, he is told that the old woman had surely forgotten; her great pain must have taken her out of her mind. For the villagers, the myth is truthful and the authentic story of the events becomes a lie. Eliade adds, not without irony, "And indeed, wasn't the myth more truthful than the story, since it gave the story a deeper, richer sound: since it revealed a tragic destiny?"

The transferring of an event across the border of legend can be labeled *mythification*. The distant kinship between mythification and what the Russian formalists called defamiliarization is worth noticing: for what else is it to project an event into a mythical territory if not to put it into a certain kind of perspective, to set it at a comfortable distance, to elevate it onto a higher plane, so that it may easily be contemplated and understood? Working on relatively recent texts such as nineteenth-century novels, the Russian formalists were mainly interested in the vividness resulting from defamiliarization, which was seen as an anticonventional device, destined to refresh the perceptual impact of the literary text on a mind accustomed to older literary procedures.[3] The vividness obtained through defamiliarization is characteristic of periods when the mechanism of literary production and consumption heavily relies on rapid obsolescence and equally rapid marketing of new designs. However, as students of archaic literature have always been aware, techniques of distancing can be developed in an entirely different way, by the use of formulaic schematism. Folk poetry, medieval epic poems, or the writings of the troubadours each offer a considerable amount of formulaic schematism.[4] Today, accustomed as we are to relate perceptual vividness to anticonventional devices, defamiliarization in particular, we have become less sensitive to the vividness resulting from conventionalist and formulaic procedures. To understand them, we must put ourselves into a more archaic frame of mind, in which the fundamental distinction is not between actual and fictional but between the insignificant and the memorable. Repetition and recognition of conventional procedures enhance the feeling of participation in a noble, durable discourse; novelty has less appeal than permanence, and the pervasive sentiment is one of stable ontological distance. Thus formulaic schematism and mythification represent different instantiations of the same basic attitude.

Though in a more liberal and modern way, these mechanisms are still at work through the sixteenth and seventeenth centuries at the level of rhetorical diction. In Christopher Marlowe's *Tamburlaine* they find subtle use as part of the dramatic technique. The rise of Tamburlaine is attributable to his rapturous speeches, which exert an instant fascination upon his followers and opponents. The Scythian thief addresses the hostile envoy, Theridamas, with highly conventional set speeches filled with hyperbolic mythological allusions:

> I hold the Fates bound fast in iron chains,
> And in my hand turn Fortune's wheel about
> And sooner shall the sun fall from his sphere
> Than Tamburlaine be slain or overcome. (I,ii,173–6)

to which Theridamas exclaims in awe:

> Not Hermes, prolocutor to the gods,
> Could use persuasions more pathetical. (I.ii.209–10)

Concerning our own attitude toward such heights of exaltation, the present meaning of "pathetical" is revealing.[5] But for Theridamas and presumably for Marlowe's public the enthusiasm was infectious, since after having heard this rhetorical appeal, the Persian lord switches sides, joining Tamburlaine's forces.

Like rhetoric and formulaic schematism, the transformation of an everyday event into legend injects vividness and significance into events and beings not so much by setting them *against* a conventional pattern as by forcefully fitting them *into* such a pattern, namely by transporting them across the borders of insignificant actuality into the memorable domain of myth. Still, remote as it may be from profane territories, the world of myths is not perceived by its users as fictional. What mythification does to beings and events is to render them distant, sometimes inaccessible, but at the same time nobly familiar, eminently visible. The heroic characters of Greek tragedies were in most cases public figures: fathers of existing cities, famous kings and criminals, notable foreigners, whose stories had been moved across the borders of legend long before the tragic poets elaborated on these plots. Today we understand fiction as a realm effectively cut off from the actual world *sub speciae veritatis;* we should not forget, however, that the separation between everyday life and these legends, these stories of famous men and women still close to the gods, enhanced rather than affected their exemplary truth.

As used here, "true" somewhat differs from its logical acceptation. A sentence $p$ is referentially true of a world $w$ if the world contains a state of affairs corresponding to $p$. For instance

(3)   Electra is Orestes' sister

is referentially true of the world of the Atrids myth, since the state of affairs "Electra is Orestes' sister" belongs to that world. By extending this notion, a sequence $p_1 + p_2 + p_3 + \ldots p_n$ is referentially true of a world $w$ if each sentence belonging to the conjunction is true of the world $w$.

(4)   Electra is Orestes' sister and Agamemnon is Electra's father and Clytemnestra kills Agamemnon

is referentially true of the world of this myth, since each of the conjuncts corresponds to a state of affairs in the mythical world. But this narrow definition does not always fit mythical situations, since myths often have variants that display various lists of states of affairs. Taking this peculiarity into account, we can define a sequence of conjoined sentences as *probabilistically* true of a world *w,* if most sentences are referentially true of *w*: a narrative of the Atrids myth would certainly be considered correct even if a few facts were missing or wrongly reported. But if the narrator failed to report that Agamemnon is Electra's father, the identity of the myth could be affected. Narratologists distinguish between basic elements of a story—*cardinal functions* in Barthes's terminology, *narremes* in Dorfman's—and less significant elements, whose presence may be dispensed with without the story's losing its coherence and identity. In such a view, it may be assumed that a sequence of conjoined sentences is *basically* true of the world *w* if all important states of affairs are represented by true sentences.

In view of the flexibility of myths, of their propensity for the development of variants, it is sufficient for narratives and plays depending on them to be basically true. Euripides' *Electra* differs in many respects from Sophocles' play or from the *Choephores;* it even on occasion openly contradicts those earlier tragedies. And, although all three texts share the same basic plot, the islands of indeterminacy gradually increase from Aeschylus to Euripides, and the weight of the basic story proportionally diminishes, while the details added by the poet become more numerous. Moreover, during this period of time the adherence of the society to the truth of the myth decreases: the process is long and leads to the loss of the privileged status enjoyed by the sacred stories and the territory they describe. Not that this territory would disappear altogether; it is too complex a structure, with too much exemplary value attached to it, for the culture to simply reject it out of hand. The myths, or at least some of them, become fictitious. The territories remain inaccessible, but for different reasons. Although the distance to myths is the distance to the sacred spaces, perhaps open to special types of travel (initiation, ritual, death), the new distance could not be dealt with by the traditional religious techniques. The gradual fictionalization of myths recalls the development of village states surrounded by the primitive forest: fictional spots develop within the mythical texture; the borders remain fuzzy, at least until recent times, since as long as myths furnish the basic truth of tragedy, fictional episodes do not drastically upset the balance. Thus the episode of the gardner in Euripides' *Electra.*

Fictional domains, therefore, are not necessarily consecrated as such from the beginning of their existence. Rather, fictionality is in most cases a historically variable property. Fictional realms sometimes arise through the extinction of the belief in a mythology; in other cases, conversely, fictionalization originates in the loss of the referential link between the characters and events described in a literary text and their real counterparts. Were the Homeric poems not assumed for a long time to speak about imaginary characters? And how often, while reading texts like the *Song of Roland* or the *Song of Igor,* do we remember that the characters are nonfictional? In a movement similar to mythification, we accept that such texts, without entirely losing the referential links to the events and characters who inhabited our world, treat their contents in a somewhat nonreferential way. The first users of such epics presumably had a different *feeling of reference* than we do, since for us medieval epics are cast in what Margolis calls a *fictional style* (1963, 1980).

Thus the frontiers of fiction separate it on one side from myth, on another from actuality. To these borders we should add the line that isolates the represented space of fiction from the spectators or readers. Accordingly, fiction is surrounded by sacred borders, by actuality borders, and by representational borders. The sacred and the representational frontiers do not surround only fiction, since the profane is distinguished from the sacred as well, and representational borders exclude us from some nonfictional domains too: the contents of a book of history are as inaccessible to its readers as those of a novel or a poem. Within these fuzzy, multiple borders, fictional territories grow in accordance with various patterns. In Greek tragedy, as we just saw, fiction developed as indeterminate spots in the texture of myth, gradually filled with new material. These, combined with the anthropocentric style of treatment initiated by Sophocles, and with the more general decay of the belief in gods, gave the tragedy its fictional aura. By the time of Euripides the borders of myth had been successfully pushed back.

A different type of fictional expansion is offered by the medieval romance. We may assume that the legendary characters present in *The Quest of the Holy Grail* were taken by the public to have actually existed. But there should be little doubt that most of the adventures narrated were destined to be understood as allegorically fictional. The structure of the text openly points to its own fictionality by the addition, after virtually every episode, of a hermeneutic reading. The strong insistence on the moral and spiritual meanings of the events suggests that they function as invented exempla. In a less open fashion, nineteenth-century historical novels often distort well-known facts for the sake of making an ideological point, a practice that has become impossible to control in our century. The strategy employed in such cases resembles that of dromocracies, or road empires (the Ottoman Empire, the British Empire), which proceed through expansion along commercial arteries without always securing dominion over the territorial hinterland. Likewise, exemplary and ideological fictions often start with a nonfictional basis, from which the construction derives a form of legitimacy; then fictional extensions are built along ideological lines, often in such a way as to leave indeterminate the frontiers between what is actual and what is not. As under road empires, territorial borders are neglected in favor of expansion along commercial arteries.

In other cases, we meet with mildly delimited territories: vaguely recognizable frontiers separate fiction from the realm of the sacred and from reality; however, there remain gaps, undefined spots, overlappings. Such seems to have been the case for many Elizabethan tragedies, *The Spanish Tragedy* for instance. In the prologue we hear the story told by the Ghost of Andrea, a Spanish nobleman killed in the war with the Portuguese. Proserpine, the Queen of Hades, allows him to attend the spectacle of his revenge, undertaken by his betrothed, Bel-Imperia. Accompanied by Revenge, an allegorical character, he sits

> down to see the mystery
> And serve for Chorus in this tragedy.   (I.i.89–90)

After each act, he and Revenge comment upon the happenings in the play. Thus the Ghost is placed on the side of the spectator: the frontier between the supernatural and the natural has been superimposed on the border between the performance and the spectator. The latter sees the play at the Ghost's side, from the perspective of the other world, as it were. But, interestingly, the setting of the play itself is less fictitious than that of the prologue, since the plot takes place in a real geographical space, which gives a certain grounding to a story that badly lacks verisimilitude. On the other hand, the afterlife scene sounds definitely fictitious, in the most conventional way, with the image of Hades being a mixture of the ancient Greek myths and the medieval Hell:

> When I was slain, my soul descended straight
> To pass the flowing stream of Acheron:
> But churlish Charon, only boatman there
> Said (I.i.18–21)

Later Andreas sees a place

> Where usurers are chok'd with melting gold
> And wantons are embraced with ugly snakes,
> And murderers groan with never-killing wounds. (I.i.67–69)

In a ironic move, through his association with Andreas' ghost, the spectator contemplates the play from the more obviously fictional side, in contrast to which the stage appears to be situated on the side of reality. A similar handling of the borders between fiction and reality, though less complex and with a different purpose, takes place in *The Taming of the Shrew*. Here again the spectator is drawn to the side of a fictional character, a maneuver that to a certain extent increases the exemplary and fictional character of the play proper.

An interesting attempt at a massive introduction of the supernatural into tragedy is the archaic-looking *Doctor Faustus* of Marlowe. In the medieval theater, the story of Creation and Salvation embodied the absolute truth in a universe with a definite structure and history. In a sense, the sacred medieval theater answered the Platonic requirement for good, truthful poetry better than any other literary project. It may also be surmised that the medieval image of the world was more or less foreign to the idea of alternative possibilities, even less to the feeling of fictional possibilities. This is perhaps why morality plays in most cases did not resort to fictive individualized characters, but instead employed abstract notions embodied as allegorical figures. Ironically, allegory becomes a way of asserting the literality of the world; everything being just the way it is, with no possible alternative, there are only two ways of representing significance: by telling stories about events and characters significant in themselves—hence the sacred stories—or by raising current, insignificant events to the level of conceptual generality, an operation that leads to exempla or, when individual determinations are lost, to the appearance of allegoric characters.

Set against this background, Marlowe's *Doctor Faustus* may be seen as an attempt to reconcile the cosmic span of medieval passion plays with the more recent use of individualized characters. This results in a plurality of registers: fiction mixes with allegory, in a tendentious way: good supernatural forces lack individuality (angels, for instance), and so do some of the evil forces, the Seven Deadly Sins, for instance. By contrast, the main representatives of evil, Mephistophilis and Lucifer, share with the human agents the privilege of possessing an individuality.

The mobility and poor determinacy of fictional frontiers is often part of a larger pattern of interaction between the domain of fiction and the actual world. Fictional domains can acquire a certain independence, subsist outside the limits of actuality, and sometimes strongly influence us, not unlike a colony established overseas that develops its own unusual constitution and later comes to affect in various ways the life of the metropolis. Such is the case of the fictions of wisdom, parables, fables, prophecies, *romans à thèse:* their fictional content hastily rebounds, so to speak, in what could be called the semantic mapping of their contents upon the actual world.[6]

Sometimes the interpretive moment is situated inside the fictional structure. *The Quest of the Holy Grail,* for instance, is organized as an incessant self-interpreting text. "In truth, Sir Knight, these adventures pertain without doubt to the Holy Grail, for everything you have told me has a meaning which I will interpret to you," says a character of the *Quest,* in a typical offer to clarify the significance of the fictional events. But a common error in interpreting literature consists in believing that all fictional constructions are destined for hermeneutic processing; this tendency may be called the *parabolic fallacy*. Do Rabelais' writings go against the teaching of the Church? Is Kafka's *Trial* a prophetic statement about subsequent trials? Or, closer to us, is Henry Miller a sexist writer? In many cases this kind of question presses the point: yes, Henry Miller is insufferably sexist. But many fictions are not planned to be profitable trading posts in wisdom trafficking. The openly playful fictions in seventeenth-century French literature, novels by Charles Sorel or Honoré d'Urfé, full of extravagant settings, characters, and actions, point toward a healthy, happy indifference to ideological interpretation. Much later, a new playful fictionality made its appearance under the sign of modernity. It took various forms, ranging from the spontaneous, sometimes naive attempts of the surrealists to the elaborate fictional mechanisms of Borges and the postmodern writers. What these undertakings have in common is the construction of fictional worlds for the sake of laying bare the properties of fiction and exploring its virtualities. Borges fills his stories with impossible objects and contradictory situations, so that no return to the metropolis is possible after "The Aleph" or "The Library of Babel." The purpose of establishing these fictional spaces is less to increase the trade in conventional wisdom than to expand our perception of fictional possibilities. Fictional colonies established as bases for traveling back and forth to the actual world must therefore be distinguished from fictional settlements founded for the sake of adventure and investigation, after burning the ships.

## Difference and Distance

Fictional borders, territories, settlements—all call for metaphoric travelers. These are the fictional heroes who visit our shores in various ways. As models they may influence our behavior as effectively as actual heroes. Did the publication of *Werther* not trigger an epidemic of suicides? Was the marital health of tens of generations not affected by Tristan and Isolde's story (if we are to believe Denis de Rougemont)? *Don Quixote* is the classic story of a life invaded by fictional characters; ironically, Quixote himself became an archetype and extensively traveled through the actual world. In addition, the peregrination of fictional characters is not restricted to the actual world, since many immigrants wander through various fictional territories other than their native land: Ulysses, Oedipus, Antigone, Faust, Don Juan.

We, too, visit fictional lands, inhabit them for a while, intermingle with the heroes. We are moved by the fate of fictional characters, since, as Kendall Walton argues, when caught up in a story, we participate in fictional happenings by projecting a fictional ego who attends the imaginary events as a kind of nonvoting member. This explanation would account for the plasticity of our relations to fiction: we are moved by the most unlikely situations and characters—Greek kings, Oriental dictators, stubborn maidens, demented musicians, men without qualities. We send our fictional egos as scouts into the territory, with orders to report back; *they* are moved, not us, they fear Godzilla and cry with Juliet, we only lend our bodies and emotions for a while to these fictional egos, just as in participatory rites the faithful lend their bodies to the possessing spirits. And just as the presence of the spirits enables the mystes to speak in tongues or foresee the future, fictional, or artistic egos are more apt to feel and express emotions than are dry, hardened actual egos. Schiller's hopes for a betterment of humanity through aesthetic education, were they not based on the presumption that after their return from travel in the realms of art, fictional egos would effectively melt back into the actual egos, sharing with them their fictional growth?

But our peregrinations are merely symbolic. Wondering about the effectiveness of fictional barriers in sealing off imaginary territories from the real ones, Kendall Walton notices that we never intrude into a play to save a damsel from the clutches of the villain; all we can do would be to interrupt the *performance* of the play. But if genuine intervention of real-world individuals in fictional contexts is excluded, psychological interaction does appear to take place. We feel, Walton says, "a psychological bond to fictions, an intimacy with them, of a kind which normally we feel only toward things we take to be actual."[7] The spectator at a horror movie is shaken by fear when he sees on the screen the monster whose nonexistence in the actual world he never doubts. He knows that the remoteness of the fictional world is such that the monster could never trespass the representational limits of the screen and invade the theater; this certitude prevents him from leaving the performance and calling the police. The spectator's fear is nonetheless quite genuine, and the question arises as to how one and the same person can experience it and not react. Walton's answer involves the fictional ego who is assigned the task of witnessing the fictional happenings and experiencing the appropriate feelings: fear, horror, pity. Any decrease of distance, according to this theory, is achieved "not by promoting fictions to our level, but by descending to theirs. More accurately, we *extend* ourselves to their level, since we do no stop actually existing when it becomes fictional that we exist" (p. 15). We pretend to inhabit fictional worlds, just as we pretend to have different destinies in daydreams, fantasizing, or various kinds of therapies.

A symmetrically similar position is proposed by Marie-Laure Ryan in a remarkable attempt to apply David Lewis' theory of conterfactuals to fiction (1980). In order to determine the truth value of counterfactual statements such as the following examples:

(5) If Napoleon did not attack England,
   (a) he would have enjoyed a long and peaceful reign
   (b) he would have been overthrown by royalists
   (c) he would have been assassinated by republicans

Lewis introduced the notion of *relative similarity* between worlds. His strategy consists in assuming that, for each such sentence, among all possible worlds accessible from the real world *w* there are worlds in which both the antecedent and the consequent hold, and worlds where the antecedent holds but the consequent does not. Let us assume, for instance, that in some worlds Napoleon did not attack England and, as a consequence, enjoyed a long and peaceful reign; in some other worlds he maintained peace with England but was soon overthrown by royalists. To assess the truth of falsehood of sentence (5a), one must evaluate the relative similarity of these worlds to the actual world. If historical research shows that there are reasons to believe that at least one of the worlds in which Napoleon keeps good relation with England and enjoys a long reign differs less from the actual world than do any of the worlds in which, in spite of peace with England, Napoleon is overthrown by the royalists, then sentence (5a) is true; in addition, (5b) can be assumed to be false. If, on the contrary, we reach the conclusion that at least one of the worlds in which Napoleon is overthrown by royalists bears more similarity to our world than do any of the worlds in which Napoleon enjoys a peaceful reign, than (5a) is false and (5b) is true.

Lewis himself and Marie-Laure Ryan extend this analysis to fictional situations. To evaluate the truth of interpretive statements such as:

(6)  Sherlock Holmes was a ladies' man

(7)  Sherlock Holmes was not interested in women

one must posit the existence of two fictional worlds: a world *a* in which all the statements found in Conan Doyle's stories about Holmes are true, (6) is true, and (7) false; and a world *b* in which the stories about Holmes are true, (6) is false, and (7) true. If we judge that the world *a* looks more similar to the real world, then (6) is true, if the world *b* resembles ours more closely, (7) is true. We have thus to assess which world is more similar to the one we inhabit: a world in which someone can behave in the way Sherlock Holmes does and still be a ladies' man, or a world constituted in such a way as to guarantee that an individual who displays Holmes's attitudes most certainly is not interested in women. The most likely answer would choose the world *b,* since in our universe dedicated bachelors like Holmes do not pay much attention to women, while a world like *a* wherein people with Holmes's behavior still nurture secret desires for the opposite sex is less like our actual world. Consequently, it is more likely that Sherlock Holmes was not a ladies' man, since "it would take a greater revision of our ideas of human psychology to say that he loves women than to say that he does not." This analysis suggests that both counterfactuals and fiction obey what Ryan calls a "principle of minimal departure," which states that "we construe the world of fiction and of counterfactuals as being the closest possible to the reality we know. This means that we will project upon the world of the statement everything we know about the real world, and that we will make only those adjustments which we cannot avoid" (1980, p. 406).

Since the principle of minimal departure appears to be shared by both counterfactuals and statements in fiction, one needs a criterion to distinguish between the two types of statements. Rather than being a discourse about a nonexisting set of worlds, Ryan suggests, literary fiction originates in the activity of impersonating, or pretending to be someone else. In this model, the author of fiction pretends to be the narrator. Her stand comes close to Searle's speech-act theory of fiction discussed above, a central assumption of which is that fictional discourse consists of pretended assertions. But while in Searle's system such assertions are attributed to a member of the actual world, say the late Mr. Tolstoy, Ryan claims that the narrator of *War and Peace* is a substitute speaker, an impersonation performed by the late Mr. Tolstoy: the narrator therefore belongs to an alternative fictional world, the world of *War and Peace*. There are more intricate situations, to be sure, such as the following lines from John Fowles's *The French Lieutenant's Woman:* "I do not know. This story I am telling you is all imagination. Those characters never existed outside my mind." To account for an utterance like this, Ryan makes the distinction between narrative discourse, undertaken by the impersonated speaker, and metanarrative comments, which belong to the author himself. Like everything literary, the distinction is not unaffected by trends and fashions. Experimentation with these roles is a favorite device of romantic authors: Jean-Paul, E. T. A. Hoffman, Nerval, Balzac. A modern master of textual orchestration, Thomas Mann, maximizes the opposition between narrator and author in *Death in Venice* and *Doctor Faustus.*[8] A fictional impersonation of the metanarrative role occurs in Iris Murdoch's *The Black Prince*.

A striking feature of Ryan's analysis is that it offers a counterpart to Walton's theory: whereas the latter describes the phenomenology of fictional reading, the former handles in similar terms the fictional writer. Caught up in the story, Walton's spectator projects a fictional ego that takes part in the imaginary happenings; symmetrically, Ryan's author impersonates a fictional speaker or writer who fully belongs to the imaginary world and in this capacity introduces the fictional beings and states of affairs to the fictional ego of the reader. The salient structure of fiction becomes apparent: the fictional exchange takes place within the secure precincts of the imaginary worlds, but it is not abruptly severed from the primary (actual) world, since fictional readers and writers emerge through impersonation by actual members of the cultural community and, as actors in the fictional system, retain most of the traits, cultural or biological, displayed by their actual bearers. Impersonation moves them across the critical distance not so much by abolishing it as by dulling their awareness of it. The principle of minimal departure is precisely a way of not acknowledging the consequences of the leap: impersonation works only so long as the fictional setting is taken seriously, imagined as real. In order to make fiction function smoothly, the reader and the author must pretend that there was no suspension of disbelief, that travel to the fictional land did not occur, and that the fictional egos have in a sense always been there, since phenomenologically they came to life together with the imaginary realm. Therefore travel to fictional lands does not necessarily entail a weakening of the usual methods of inference, common-sense knowledge, and habitual emotions. When differences occur with respect to acquired knowledge or emotional habits, they have to be processed in the same way as non-fictional fresh information. The impersonated fictional ego examines the territories and events around him with the same curiosity and eagerness to check the interplay between sameness and difference, as does any traveler in foreign lands. Fictional distance appears to boil down to difference and, in order to be manageable, difference must be kept to a minumum.

## Fictional Modes and Cultural Economies

But is reduction of distance to difference always possible? Both Walton and Ryan treat impersonation as the key act in passing from actuality to the fictional realm. Impersonation serves the purpose of changing the ontological setting more than any other means, to the point that sometimes the same text can be interpreted as fictional or not, according to the presence or absence of impersonation, the author's or the reader's. But can we describe the metamorphosis from actuality to fiction just by measuring the differences between the point of departure and the target world? Are these differences merely quantitative, as Lewis' notion of closeness between worlds seems to entail? Consider a contemporary reader, reasonably educated, interested in literature, and willing to venture into various fictional spaces. It is reasonable to assume that novels like Saul Bellow's *Herzog* or William Styron's *Sophie's Choice* would require very little displacement, since to understand them it suffices to accept the fictionality of the text. Charlotte Bronte's *Jane Eyre* would ask for more; in order to under-

stand nineteenth-century fiction, our reader must make a supplementary effort: his impersonation would thus become more laborious
and involve either the activation of background knowledge, if available, or a more strenuous exertion in grasping the significant details
and constructing an adequate frame of reference. *Gulliver's Travels*
necessitates still more willingness to reshape the usual frames of reference. On this scale, *The Quest of the Holy Grail* stands even farther
from our reader's actual world, but not so far as, say, an Australian
myth. Such a scale indicates that the remoteness of fictional worlds
from the reader's inhabited world does not involve just the amount
of new information absorbed, for it may well be that in order to
assimilate a text like *Herzog* or *Sophie's Choice* the reader must accept
more information than in the case of, say, *The Quest of the Holy Grail.*
Contemporary young readers could find it more taxing to adjust their
frames of reference to the images of prewar Poland or the description
of Sophie's life at Auschwitz than to integrate smoothly a mildly
fabulous story about knights, hermits, sin, and purity. But obviously
this does not mean that such readers find *The Quest* more like our
world than *Sophie's Choice*. The frames of reference of the fictional
text do not merely include the sum of new states of affairs but also
the general quality of the alternate world. To project a fictional ego
who would optimally understand *The Quest,* the reader would have
to achieve a much more radical impersonation than for *Sophie's Choice,*
since he would have to pretend that basic laws of the universe undergo
a change. Although the details provided in *The Quest* are not numerous, they suggest a different chain of beings, another history,
another geography, new epistemic regularities, unexpected moral
maxims. The impersonating effort qualitatively increases with historical and cultural distance: in order to send a well-prepared fictional
ego to *The Quest* or *Gulliver's Travels,* we have to adjust some essential
shifters of our frames of reference

Northrop Frye's theory of fictional modes (1967) offers a differentiated account of such adjustments. Based on the Aristotelian criterion of the elevation of the characters, it distinguishes myths, which
tell stories about beings superior in kind to other men and their
environment; romance, which stages heroes superior in degree to men
and the environment (legends and some folktales are included here);
the high mimetic mode, which deals with heroes superior in degree
to other men but not to the environment; the low mimetic mode, to
which belong characters equal to their kind and environment; and
the ironic mode, which deals with those characters who are inferior

in power or intelligence to the spectator. In addition, Frye suggests a correlation between this typology and the history of Western fiction: a slow evolution makes literature shift from the highest to the lowest modes. From mythical texts to Christian romance, Renaissance high mimetic mode, middle-class preference for the low mimetic fiction, and the modern ironic tone, a series of conspicuous transitions takes place in what Frye calls the "foreground" of literary habits.

Such shifts notwithstanding, a variety of modes can be found in virtually every culture. Pre-medieval literature included not only myths but also sagas, some of which resembled romance, while others narrated high mimetic stories about dignified founders. In archaic cultures, folktales do not by necessity belong to romance only: it is not difficult to notice that in Aarne-Thompson's classification supernatural tales are merely one of the numerous categories of folktales. Some of the romantic folktales may be classified as high mimetic (AT 850–899, and in particular AT 930–949, among which one finds AT 930 The Prophecy, and AT 931 Oedipus); animal stories are low mimetic, while humorous stories about tricksters or fools display ironic traits. All periods of Western culture, ours included, appear to consume considerable amounts of products that belong to each of these five modes; healthy narrative cultures need a good diversity of fictional modes and situate their fictional worlds at various distances. It can, on the other hand, be argued that even if consumption covers all modes, production of the highest modes gradually diminishes. But it does not disappear altogether. Even in our reputedly ironic century, romance can be recognized in fantastic literature, or in religious fictions such as *L'Annonce faite à Marie* by Claudel, *Murder in the Cathedral* by T. S. Eliot, or *Dialogue des Carmélites* by Bernanos. High mimetic texts abound: *Remembrance of Things Past* is, in a sense, the story of a hero who proves himself through art stronger than his human environment. Mixture of modes often favors the presence of the high mimetic register: Mann's tetralogy *Joseph and His Brothers* is based on a combination of irony and genuine sublimity; but did not all Elizabethan dramatists already employ heavy irony to ease the high mimetic tension? We tend to exaggerate our period's involvement with low and ironic modes, and its alleged withdrawal from the sacred and from myth.

A typogical distinction will perhaps clarify the question: to *self-contained* fictional economies, I would oppose *nostalgic* or *import-dependent* systems. Self-contained cultures mostly consume their own fictional production, keeping imports to a minimum, or attentively adapting foreign products to local needs. Archaic cultures and the West European medieval period are examples of self-contained fictional commonwealths. With a set of religious myths and a diversified endowment of folktales, any rural culture can satisfy its fictional needs and play with all the above-noted modes. Also the late Middle Ages enjoyed a full range of fictional modes, all produced domestically, from passion plays to comic theater.

Nostalgic cultures, in contrast, massively import fiction, looking for merchandise in bygone epochs or faraway lands. This may happen either because the domestic production is insufficient (Byzantine literature) or because the needs become extremely diversified and, without competing with the consumption of new fictional texts, an interest develops in genuine foreign or antique pieces. During the Romantic and post-Romantic periods, which constitute the best available examples of nostalgic systems, the widening of the historical horizon may have helped the low mimetic modes to prevail in so far as production of new texts was concerned. For why should nineteenth- and twentieth-century writers bother with concocting high mimetic texts, tragedies about gods, kings, and heroes for instance, when the Greek texts can so well answer this need? What is the rationale behind writing *L'Annonce faite à Marie,* when similar heights can be reached through reading or attending performances of medieval miracle plays? If, just like Claudel's text, these run the risk of sometimes sounding awkward, they can at least be forgiven on historical grounds.

In the end, one feels tempted to ask whether a single criterion of distance and difference is sufficient, and whether it is enough to speak in terms such as superiority in nature or in degree. For, aside from the intrinsic separation between the world of the reader and the fictional world, there might be other principles at work. If the test of distance is impersonation, its measure must be the impersonating *effort,* the tension needed for the ego to project its fictional surrogate. And while it is reasonable to assume that this effort has to be increased or diminished according to the "objective" distance between the world of the spectator and the fictional world, it is equally probable that the style of fictional presentation can independently add or decrease the *perceived* distance. The same story about heroes and gods can be framed as a solemn development that takes place in a realm drastically cut off from ours, or as a lower mimetic story focusing on the anthropomorphic traits of these exceptional creatures. Variation of this kind can be noticed, again, in the transition from the more archaic style of Aeschylus' tragedies to the modern tone of Euripides' plays.

Or, on the contrary, stories about the most common individuals are sometimes framed in such a way as to maximize the distance and to require a considerable effort of impersonation—thus Büchner's *Woyzzek* or Bataille's "Madame Edwarda." The various techniques of fragmentation, illogical sequencing, purple passages expressing anxiety and delirium, and the tragic ending suggest a world of mystery and ritual, better fitted for supernatural characters than for the wretched protagonists of these texts. In such cases we do not consistently apply the minimal departure principle, since we do not want to give *Woyzzek* the closest interpretation to the reality we know. On the contrary, when confronted with fictions of this kind, we seem to anticipate a maximal departure and to look anxiously after its signs. Mimetic principles are supplemented with antimimetic expectations. There are worlds where Sherlock Holmes, while behaving as he does in Conan Doyle's stories, is a secret but compulsive admirer of women, and the novels describing these worlds would be easy to understand, if enough clues were offered that would enable us to figure out an *optimal departure* by virtue of which we would consistently make sense out of unusual states of affairs.

The perceptual adventures of the fictional ego equally depend on the friendliness of the text. Some works helpfully assist ther readers to orient themselves and adjust their fictional egos to the alternate world: there is little doubt in *Tom Jones* or in *Vanity Fair* about the kind of world we are expected to attend. But not so in *The Quest of the Holy Grail* or in Kafka's *Castle,* texts that introduce us to puzzling worlds, lead us to inadequate hypotheses, and encourage us to hesitate and to project a perplexed fictional ego, unsure of its ability to make sense of the events it witnesses. It is incomprehensible why all passive agents in *The Quest* know so well the future and the meaning of each event, while those who act sink, as it were, into a state of ignorance that dissipates as soon as the agent sees the action of someone else, whereby he instantly acquires the gift of prophecy. In Kafka's *Castle* constraints on the fictional ego are equally disturbing: contradictory clues seem to suggest alternatively that the world we attend is sometimes similar to ours and sometimes obeys an alien logic. Too well-structured to be simply oneiric, too realistic to accept a mythic framework, the nature of the fictional surroundings remains elusive. One can hardly think of an optimal-departure metrics that would consistently work in all circumstances of the novel. Distance indicators are willfully jammed, leaving indeterminate the choice between familiarity and infinite remoteness.

## The Size of Fictional Worlds

Chekhov would probably have thought that a confused and dying man counting his few belongings, trying to remember past events, provided an excellent theme for a short story. The destiny of a law student in Bombay, caught in the midst of the fighting between Moslems and Hindus, looking for a thief woman from Palanpur, taking part in a conspiracy in Katmandu, attracted to a mysterious quest for a personal savior, would have certainly been in Kipling's eyes a beautiful colorful subject for a novel. The first theme is the subject to Beckett's novel *Malone Dies,* while the second abstracts Borges' seven-page story "The Approach to al-Mu'tasim." We cannot prejudge the size of a fictional world from the dimensions of the text speaking about it. Not unlike natural languages, in which a given syntactic category, say the subject slot in a sentence like "————sneezed," can be filled by segments of various lengths, from single words (he, she, John) to interminable noun phrases including numerous embedded clauses, textual manifestations are subject to expansion and contraction. Hence the possibility of abstracting a story, of expanding a narrative idea, of deriving a long flowery play from a short myth (Corneille's *Oedipe*), or a relatively short play from a lengthy novel. The classic question "why is a short story short?" and its possible counterpart "why is a long novel long?" cannot be answered in a purely referential way, by making the dimensions of the text depend on those of the world about which it speaks. The fictional universe of "The Approach to al-Mu'tasim" may exceed in size the worlds of *Remembrance of Things Past.* Nevertheless, an evaluation of the size of the worlds in question plays an important role in the understanding of fictional texts.

Although they do not agree on how to characterize it, possible-worlds philosophers include the notion of size in their definition of worlds. We have already seen that Plantinga equates worlds with maximal states of affairs, so that, for any state of affairs S, the world either includes S or its negation S'. Should we distinguish between what is "in fact" part of a fictional world and the parts of it that are of interest to the reader? Or should we rather assume that fictional worlds, as internal models, must limit themselves to what is of concern to the reader? Obviously, if the latter course is chosen, we do not want fictional worlds to be maximal, since we are not interested in what lurks behind a limited circle of light and the penumbra surrounding it. The most encompassing fictional world does not extend beyond that circle, and when reading *Don Quixote* we care little about states of affairs related, say, to Brazil; nor do we worry about astrology when engulfed in Marcel's unhappy infatuation with Albertine. The interesting distinction between *homogeneous* and *heterogenous* systems of possible worlds made by Stephen Körner can help conceptualize this limitation (1973). Körner sets apart homogeneous systems, in which all worlds share the same categorial structure, from heterogenous systems, in which the worlds belonging to the system enjoy different categorial structures. Since most fictions involve mixed systems, containing actual, possible, and fictive elements, they must be classified as heterogeneous; more important, it is appropriate to grant to these systems some form of categorial heterogeneity because we do not want inference to spread indiscriminately across fictional worlds. Indeed, it would be inappropriate to include all laws of nature in any group of fictional worlds. Are the laws of thermodynamics a part of the worlds of *Les Liaisons dangereuses?* or, to take an example subsequent to their discovery, are they of any import in the world of Böll's *Portrait of Group with Lady?* Some form of gradual opacity to inference, some increasing resistance to maximal structures, must be at work in most fictional worlds, keeping them from expanding indefinitely along irrelevant lines. In this respect fictional worlds again display an archaic trait; they resemble the worlds of common sense, of premodern, uneducated common sense; worlds where a highly structured central area is surrounded by increasingly dark, fuzzy spaces.

A different approach to the size of possible worlds is offered by M. J. Creswell's definition of a world as a set of basic particular situations (1972). These situations, Creswell explains, must be thought of "as rather like the atomic facts of the logical atomists in that a basic particular situation is something which may or may not be present without affecting any other basic particular situations . . . What sort of thing we take them to be will of course depend on a thoroughgoing analysis of the language we are interested in" (p. 135). In Creswell's own example, the role of basic particular situations is played by space-time points, a choice that allows the world to reach any size, from a single space-time point, to a maximal set of particular situations. It can be pointed out in passing that Creswell's stand works well for the materialist philosopher, since it restricts possible worlds to fragments and rearrangements of the actual world. By positing a kind of "real" inventory of atoms and allowing only those alternatives to the actual world that are made up of atoms traceable to this inventory, combinatorialism displays a firm commitment to reality. In relation to fictional beings and worlds, combinatorialism is a respectable position, perennially defended by classic and realist critics. What is Pegasus if not a combination of a horse and a pair of wings? Nevertheless, combinatorialism is not a compelling theory, and we may well accept Creswell's notion of worlds as small as required, without restricting them to combinations of actual spatial-temporal points. The ontology of fictional worlds is not by necessity combinatorialist, even if various periods or trends have adopted a conspicuous combinatorialist stand: chimerae were indeed reducible to real elements, just as Archimboldo's portraits decompose into fruit and vegetables; and do not eighteenth- and nineteenth-century realist novels programmatically limit their ontology to kinds of beings belonging to the actual world? But even these examples show that more complex varieties of combinatorialism go beyond space-time points and use as building blocks natural kinds, social types and roles, and so on. Obviously, space-time points are insufficient for realist and irrealist fiction alike. How could we account, for example, for an entity like Borges' Aleph in terms of space-time points? This impossible object is not composed of parts; within it part and whole meet, including everything past and present within a unifying perception:

> On the back of the step, toward the right, I saw a small iridescent sphere of almost unbearable brillance. At first I thought it was revolving; then I realized that this movement was an illusion created by the dizzying world it bounded. The Aleph's diameter was probably little more than an inch, but all space was there, actual and undiminished. Each thing (a mirror's face, let us say) was infinite things, since I distinctly saw it from every angle of the universe. I saw the teeming sea; I saw daybreak and nightfall; I saw the multitudes of America . . . I saw the Aleph from every point and angle, and in the Aleph I saw the earth and in the earth the Aleph and in the Aleph the earth; I saw my own face and my own bowels; I saw your face; and I felt dizzy and wept, for my eyes had seen that secret and conjectured object whose name is common to all men but which no man has looked upon—the unimaginable universe.

The Aleph is a mystic object about which one can neither speak properly nor keep silent: it belongs to the infinite class of ultra-Meinongian objects that not only do not exist in any current sense of the verb "to exist" but cannot be adequately described in any conceivable language. God and his ten Sephiroth are such entities. Says Borges, alluding to his despair as a writer:

All language is a set of symbols whose use among its speakers assumes a shared past. How, then, can I translate into words the limitless Aleph, which my floundering mind can scarcely encompass? Mystics, faced with the same problem, fall back on symbols: to signify the godhead, one Persian speaks of a bird that somehow is all birds; Alanus de Insulis, of a sphere whose center is everywhere and circumference nowhere; Ezekiel, of a four-faced angel who at one and the same time moves east and west, north and south.

The theory of fiction is too complex for combinatorialism.

The question of the relative size of worlds and texts must therefore be tackled independently of the building blocks that make up fictional worlds. A possible approach would consist in assuming that the worlds of fiction come in various sizes, all adequately represented by texts and well perceived by the penetrating eye of the reader or spectator. Under this assumption, the size of a fictional world is directly related to textual size: the fictional states of affairs are those described or easily inferred from the sentences of the text. Problems of inference set aside, this view presents certain advantages, simplicity not being the smallest. It provides for a straightforward answer to the question "why are short stories short?" This undoubtedly corresponds to an intuition shared by readers and critics: short stories usually deal with tiny fragments of life, while epics and novels describe large, richly furnished universes. Fictional genres, one can surmise, specialize in certain ranges of world dimensions. That in a given period dramas, poems, or novels tend not to trespass certain textual proportions can thus be explained by genre preference for worlds of determinate sizes. Renaissance tragedy rarely sets in motion more than two full plots, each involving a few characters. *King Lear,* one of the most complicated machineries of the period, makes use of about twelve to fifteen active characters, depending on the way we count them. *Antony and Cleopatra* is more populous, containing twenty to thirty individualized characters. Both plays are relatively long, containing many changes in place and fortune, but they do not exceed the limits of the genre. When in the second half of the seventeenth century taste drastically changed, and under French influence tragedy was reduced to the bare essentials, the new textual dimensions did not shrink to a radically different range. Between a Shakespearian tragedy of over 3000 lines and a play by Racine of over 2000 lines the difference is not excessive. A referential explanation would point to the lack of disparity between the universe depicted by the two trends. Contrary to a widespread belief and the principle of unity of action, Racine's tragedies handle two plots, well embedded within one another, such that the character who in the main plot is the target of a tragic passion himself nurtures unreciprocated love feelings in a secondary plot: thus Junie between Nero and Britannicus, Bajazet between Roxane and Athalide, Hippolyte between Phèdre and Aricie. The number of characters does not exceed eight, confidants included; the place of action remains confined to the fatidic antechamber Barthes described so vividly, but it entertains multiple links with the outside world. If there is a difference in magnitude between the universe of *King Lear* and that of *Phèdre,* it is a moderate one and relates, as will be seen later, to variation in textual density and orchestration. Textual dimension appears to reflect faithfully the change in referential scope.

This stand unfortunately works only in those cases in which the eye of the reader or spectator remains unmoved, like a camera lens without a zoom device. If, like the camera of the earliest movies, textual selection of narrated events always proceeds along the same principles and quotas, if emphasis remains constant and perceptual proximity does not vary, then obviously the amplitude of the fictional world is the only variable determining textual expanse. But if this ever happened in fictional literature, it must certainly have been for limited periods of time. Even though the monotony of certain medieval narratives reminds us of the perceptual immobility of a static camera, this situation presents itself as an exception. The scale of the text appears rather to relate to the *perception* of dimension; long novels develop a feeling of breadth, short stories one of fleeting immediacy. The average length of a genre may thus obey psychological constraints: a play cannot usually sustain the audience's attention for more than a couple of hours; a movie's duration depends on the eye's tolerance to strain. Therefore, far from originating in the dimensions of the fictional world, textual amplitude may well reflect perceptual and generic constraints.

An alternate model would then posit an always maximal fictional world, in the fashion of Plantinga, out of which diversely organized texts tailor to size various referential domains. The maximal fictional world can either be taken to be similar to the actual world in accordance with the principle of minimal departure, or it can be situated at an *optimal distance,* calculated according to specific clues offered by the text. We may visualize it as a general fictional domain where humans send their fictions to live, or grant it cultural individuality as the imaginary stronghold of a given period, or else we can give each fictional text the right to posit its own fictional world. The choice bears upon the crucial question of inference and its projected power. If fictive worlds constitute a transcultural homogeneous space, inference would be allowed to spread without adequate barriers; characters from various quarters would counterintuitively mix with one another; the laws of nature would retroactively apply, and fictional privacy would constantly be violated. These are unpleasant consequences.

To postulate unified fictional fields according to historical and cultural periods is a preferable choice, and one that fits in well with the Hegelian tradition and recent developments in historical anthropology. Historians of mentalities have shown how societies tend to develop characteristic imaginary spaces that inform both social life and cultural production. Members of the society judge fictional texts in accordance with the prevailing general laws of the imaginary; conversely, literary fiction helps the development of the imaginary, either by offering it a powerful confirmation or by contributing to its gradual transformation. A telling example is the birth of Purgatory in the twelfth century, analyzed by Jacques Le Goff. The gradual formation of an imaginary space where the redeemable soul spends a limited time cleansing itself from venial sins was related to well-entrenched social rites such as prayers and intercessions for the dead, to the daily activity of the imaginary (dreams and visions), and to the theological development of Christian doctrine. This innovation brought with it a profound change in the perception of temporality; on the road between this world and eternity, Purgatory became the transitional place where time still counted. It ambiguously contributed to the mitigation of Divine Justice. Sometimes perceived as a territory of hope, it made transgressions appear less radical: once their pains commuted from Hell to Purgatory, usurers began to thrive, helping the growth of capitalism. As a reaction to potential permissiveness, the Church gradually "infernalized" Purgatory, rendering its pains utterly severe. It is only against this background that we can understand Dante's *Purgatory,* written approximately a century after the stabilization of the new place. The poem played a considerable role in the implementation of the new spatial structure that was destined to be universally represented and celebrated by religious art between the fifteenth and the nineteenth centuries.

Still there are situations in which it does not make much sense to assume a culturally unified world of the imagination, variously referred to by texts of different sizes. Contemporary science fiction, for instance, often posits entirely new worlds that can in no way be reduced to one all-encompassing fictional base. In such contexts it would perhaps serve us better to assume that each text or family of texts posits an idiosyncratic fictional world *and* sheds light on a fragment of it. *Rendez-vous with Rama* by Arthur Clarke refers to a world different from that of *Solaris* by Stanislas Lem; in addition, each text concentrates only on some parts of its world, and we never find out where Rama comes from or what is the nature of the mysterious ocean on Solaris. Such contexts do not weaken the notion of the collective imagination, since the very existence and success of modern science fiction is conditioned by the rise of a new collective imaginary. The example only shows the need to distinguish between collective imagination as a general frame of reference and fictional worlds proper.

A third model would assume that fictional worlds, without reaching maximality, possess stable dimensions, variously suggested by the literary texts that describe them. This model might occasion new questions: How are fictional worlds focused upon? How do texts suggest various world horizons? Are there referential angles of view different from the points of view described by narratology and the rhetoric of fiction? To answer the last question we need to distinguish sharply between epistemic and rhetorical strategies, on the one hand, and techniques of world presentation on the other. Most procedures analyzed by Wayne Booth, Gerard Genette, Dorrit Cohn, and other theorists are ways of introducing the reader to the narrated world. They represent encoding techniques, whose purpose is to render narration attractive, surprising, impossible to abandon. But aside from discursive techniques deployed along the temporal axis of the text, there is a group of relevant factors that becomes visible only after the end of the reception process. For instance, Joseph Frank and other critics have described the notion of *spatial form,* whose global configuration cannot be grasped in its entirety at any moment during the act of reading.[9] Also we fully understand the properties of fictional worlds, size included, only after having completed the reading of the text.

Since in this model worlds do not need to be maximal, stable extratextual limits do not entail completeness or consistency. The text of *Madame Bovary* introduces us to a fictional world whose amplitude is relatively independent of the size of the text, for, if we delete from each chapter one or two relatively unimportant sentences, the text would be shorter while the size of the projected world would remain unchanged. But the projection has limits: when measuring the relevant enclosure, we must at some point stop making inferences and importing extratextual knowledge. The limit varies typologically, since fictional universes differ in *scope* and *openness to extratextual information*.

With respect to scope, we can construct a scalar typology ranging between maximal fictional universes, such as the universe of the *Divine Comedy,* and minimal universes, such as the world of *Malone Dies.* The well-documented transition toward ever smaller universes that has accompanied the evolution of Western fictional writing may well be connected to the previously noted decrease in distance: closer views tend to be limited in scope. Such sweeping generalizations must of course be qualified: the *Divine Comedy* coexisted with the *Vita Nuova* and medieval farce, while nineteenth-century realism gave rise to gigantic fictional enterprises. But between the *Divine Comedy* and *La Comédie humaine,* the radical expansion of nonliterary discourses about the world rendered obsolete any attempt at building maximal fictional worlds. Nowadays, only inventive science-fiction writers still dare attempt the creation of entire universes.

Diversity derives as well from permeability with respect to extratextual information. Works like the *Divine Comedy* seem to be composed with the purpose of favoring commentary and detailed linking to contemporary philosophy, theology, history, and science. Reference to Thomas Aquinas, historical events in Florence, medieval science, and political wisdom are built into the text and belong to the calculated general effect. Encyclopedic and satiric texts are highly permeable, and so are their modern counterparts, the realist and philosophical novel. When reading Balzac or Mann, it makes sense constantly to remember social factors, historical events, and philosophical trends. On the contrary, romance, tragedy, and twentieth-century "transparent minds" narratives tend deliberately to push the empirical world away, and to concentrate on the inner logic of the fictional worlds, rendered more or less impermeable to extratextual information. Relevant as Aquinas' ideas on various matters may be for the understanding of Dante's poem, they little serve the reader of *The Quest of the Holy Grail* or *Morte d'Arthur.* Knowledge of Schopenhauer's and Nietzsche's writings helps to perfect our grasp of *The Magic Mountain* but not necessarily of *Molloy* or *La Route des Flandres.*

The relationship between world dimensions and text dimensions determines what might be called the *referential density* of a text. If we allow textual amplitude to vary while keeping the dimensions of the fictional world constant, the longer text will appear more diluted than the shorter. A literary competition on the theme of the Boston Tea

Party may occasion a ten-page witty account of the events as well as a fifteen-hundred-page novel that calmly includes detailed descriptions and interior monologues. Which of the two submissions should get the prize? Does either of the two attain the *optimal* compactness? To render less vague the impression that a text efficiently leads to its set of worlds, we could speak of *relative* density, in whose assessment we may include the relation between texts and worlds, and such variables as the external information needed to understand the text, its narrative crowding, the ratio between action and description, and the epistemic paths chosen by the text.

The need for external information, we have already seen, increases the porosity of a text; writers conspicuously keep their texts open to outside data, often falling into the trap of fastidiousness. Balzac's lengthy descriptions of houses and furniture, his penetrating remarks on the legal and financial system of early nineteenth-century France, arouse the interest of the sociologically oriented reader, but for the rest they may appear excessive. Similarly, the endless intellectual joust between Naphta and Settembrini in *The Magic Mountain* sometimes makes the novel sound unnecessarily inflated. One can argue that these examples involve writers who passionately wove referential threads into their fictional constructions. But beyond individual preferences, porosity to actual world information is a recurrent quality, imperiously required by shifts in taste. Romantic novelists felt responsible for bringing back to collective memory forgotten institutions and customs. The secrets of navigation haunted the American imagination of the nineteenth century, as witnessed by the abundance of maritime information in Poe's or Melville's prose. The same century saw the development of exotic novels, thriving on descriptions of faraway places, frontier culture, marginal social groups. Other moments in history have preferred less permeable fictions: three decades ago the *nouveau roman* attempted to reduce the links between the texts and the world outside to a minimum; hence the impression of density left by the texts of Claude Simon or Robert Pinget.

In addition to documentary incursions, the relative density of texts varies with their degree of narrative agglomeration. Narratives or plays can combine two, three, or more plots, the number of characters involved in each can be increased, the events complicated. Between a no-event text like Beckett's *Happy Days* and *Tom Jones* there is a continuum of solutions, making use of variously sized narrative crowds. Plots can be analyzed into moves, which are independent actions, each having an impact on the development of the plot (Pavel, 1985b). The ratio between the number of moves in a plot and the length of the text determines the narrative or dramatic tempo; a lively text deploys a high number of moves within a concise development, say Spanish picaresque novels and their French and English descendants. During the nineteenth century, narrative tempo gradually slowed. Without being much shorter than *Tom Jones, Vanity Fair* contains considerably less movement. At the beginning of this century, narrative flow reached a genuine impasse: the heroes of *Remembrance of Things Past* or *The Man Without Qualities* need hundreds of pages to make a few moves that would have required Tom Jones just a chapter or two.

Groups of characters sharing the same moves form narrative or dramatic domains. In *King Lear,* for instance, after the partition of the kingdom, Lear, Kent, and Cordelia belong to the same dramatic domain, while Goneril, Regan, their husbands, and Edmund constitute the opposite domain. Later the configuration changes, as Goneril and Regan start to fight while Albany and Edgar join the domain of Lear by virtue of their inimity to Edmund. I would call *narrative* or *dramatic orchestration* the relationship between the number of domains and that of the corresponding characters. A text like *King Lear* that handles between three and four domains, each populated by three to six characters, is felt as considerably more reverberating than a work that includes just one or two characters in each domain. Classical tragedy, Greek and French, excels in subdued orchestration. Racine limits his dramatic domains to a few characters: in *Phèdre* the main protagonist's domain consists only in the unfortunate queen and her servant Oenone. But if one takes into account that in a classical tragedy confidants do not play a structurally independent part, representing no more than an extension of the main protagonist, the economy of means appears even more striking. These double-star structures that pair Phèdre and Oenone, Hippolyte and Théramène, Aricie and Ismène, agreeably populate the stage, without adding any strain to the plot: as in a *viola d'amore,* only one set of strings actively contributes to the sound. Preferring a richer narrative orchestration, the nineteenth-century realist novel surrounds the main actors with a score of lesser characters, each endowed with some initiative of his own; the alliance systems and the regimentation of characters within domains is less drastic than in seventeenth- and eighteenth-century novels. A comparison between the domains of *Les Liaisons dangereuses* and that of *Splendeurs et misères des courtisanes* shows the technical evolution: while in Laclos' text characters are firmly attached to their domains, leaving them rarely and only under the pressure of love or hate, in Balzac's story the alliance system acquires a distinct fluidity: Rubempré, Vautrin, Delphine, and Nucingen never stabilize their allegiances and adroitly travel from one domain to another, according to their complex interests.

At a level closer to the textual arrangement, the well-known distinction between *telling* and *showing* contributes in its own way to the effect of density. Telling increases the compactness of a text, since it saves space and helps the crowding of lengthy events into rapid narrative segments. One of the most appealing features of French short novels such as *La Princesse de Clèves, Manon Lescaut, Adolphe, Le Diable au corps, La Chute,* and *Le Coup de grâce* is the preponderance of telling over showing: it fosters a sense of detachment and mastery over large developments of human destiny. It also gives readers the feeling that their investment of attention gets an optimal return. In such texts, no detail can be passed over without important loss of information; it follows that the control of decoding reaches maximal efficiency. Guided with a firm hand by the author, the reader has to accept discipline, since the effort of attention is so well rewarded by the enhanced relevance of the text.

Last but not least, relative density depends on the epistemic paths that lead to the worlds of the text. *Adolphe* not only tells more than it shows but also tells according to an abstract moralizing system of categories. This choice enables the author to save on details of the action; the tone of moral generalization concurs to suggest rapidity and control, hence textual density. The procedure is intensified in Borges' "Lottery at Babylon," where a maximally dense text calmly describes an allegory of the entire world in a few pages. A different approach concentrates on significant details, insisting on the process of naive perception and leaving the elaboration of more abstract moral conclusions to the reader. Tolstoy's technique of defamiliarization, analyzed by the Russian formalists, requires a patient regard for appearances: more elaborated, such texts are less compact, since the ratio text-to-world does not deliberately favor the latter. Through a similar technique, short stories maximize the fragmentation effect: by concentrating upon a piece of the world, they place it under a strong, unusual light. A last category includes redundant texts, from the jocular prose of Rabelais to contemporary avant-garde writers who play with the signifier. The information density of such texts slides toward zero: the brew bubbles for its own sake, as it were, and textual size and density cast themselves free from referential moorings.

## Incomplete Worlds, Ritual Emotions

Allowance for fictional worlds of various sizes implies that they may be rich or poor, more or less comprehensive. Philosophers who relate comprehensiveness to ease of inference believe that the states of affairs comprised in fictional worlds must be fairly sizable, since they should include "not only what the author indicates, but also whatever is required (entailed) by which he implicates."[10] The laws of nature that are not specifically contradicted by the text belong to its worlds: a few notorious cases aside, the autokopros Joseph Andrews included, every child born in fiction having been engendered by a human father, there is no reason to doubt this regularity as long as the text signals no exception. If, however, the text does report such an anomaly, then, assuming that the laws of logic still govern, if not fiction itself at least our understanding of it, we may appeal to what possible-worlds philosophers have called "small miracles."

We can imagine, for instance, a world in which Notre Dame de Paris is covered with blue paint. While everything else would preserve the properties it possesses in the actual world, with the laws of nature and the normal causal chains maintained, a small local change, some-what miraculous, modifies just and only the color of that venerable building. Similarly, the world of Balzac may be understood as the world of early and mid-nineteenth-century France, slightly modified by the addition of about three thousand characters. That these con-form surprisingly well to the general trends of French society of the time is such a deliberate goal of Balzac's successful project that for the sociologically minded reader the actual nonexistence of Rastignac, Rubempré, Vautrin, or Birotteau may appear to be a mere accident. These characters, one may surmise, display every trait that their actual counterparts would possess, except existence. Hence why would Ras-tignac's or Vautrin's emergence in a world otherwise identical with nineteenth-century France amount to anything more than a small miracle? On the other hand, Balzac's world being blessed with thou-sands of such miracles, the very magnitude of the project vindicates the attribute of "visionary," ascribed to Balzac by Béguin, or even the title of "God the Father" generously offered by Thibaudet. For would not such magnitude entail more than just local changes in an otherwise faithful representation of the actual nineteenth-century France?

Conversely, would we interpret a fictional world in which a child has been engendered not by a human father but by a divinity as identical in all respects to the actual world, except for the limited modification attributed to a small miracle?

If we believe that nineteenth-century France was a given and that Balzac did not perform anything but bring into fictional existence hundreds of characters against the firmly established background of that given, does not his feat still deserve the admiration of Béguin and Thibaudet? But even if we take the opposite course, and assume that nineteenth-century France is not a given and that Balzac's world does not differ from *it* by a multitude of miraculous births, his achievement bears upon the actual world: in some very significant respects our image of nineteenth-century France has at least partly been shaped by Balzac's works, and his writings enjoyed a much wider circulation and success than those of many a lesser-skilled historian. Perhaps it is not even a matter of genuine competition: Balzac's version may have struck nearly everyone as being so dense and convincing that no rival account had to be considered. Perhaps it occurred to Balzac's readers that the *Comédie humaine* was bound to be true, true as a well-structured whole, wherein Vautrin and Goriot and Grandet belong just as legitimately as the intricate descriptions of Paris streets or the endless references to Napoleonic civil law. Likewise, children engendered by divinities do not signal local miracles in otherwise normal worlds; they tend rather to emerge in places considerably different from the actual ones, and their presence reveals to us the essential saliency of the world in question, a world open to hierophany, prodigies, and saviors.

Thus, whether fictional worlds represent credible accounts of our universes or give a version of universes contaminated by radical otherness, they tend to blur the distinction between laws in force in the actual world and small miracles specific to fiction. The Balzac world version would be equally affected by the discovery that Napoleonic civil law was in fact quite different from its description in the novels, and by the realization that all texts and passages referring to Vautrin were interpolated later by some other writer. Truths copied by the author and invented characters belong in an often indistinguishable fashion to the fictional world.

But does this not entail that, conversely, one should refrain from *adding* to this world facts and laws that are not alluded to in the text, just as no one ever thought of adding to the world of Balzac all ancestors of Vautrin, although their existence is somewhat entailed by the appearance of Vautrin. Instead of overcrowding fictional worlds with scores of entailed (or required) facts and laws, we are free to make the opposite choice, which is to limit these worlds to what is described, unambiguously implied, or alluded to in the text.

This option is not without its problems. Since the property of having a cousin is not explicitly attributed to Vautrin in Balzac's novels, it means that based on textual evidence, unless we postulate an improbable law such as "every character in the *Comédie humaine* has at least one cousin," one cannot decide which of the two sentences "Vautrin has a cousin" and "Vautrin does not have a cousin" is true in the fictional world under scrutiny. Hence the world in question is incomplete.

For several writers, incompleteness constitutes a major distinctive feature of fictional worlds.[11] About complete worlds, one can decide whether for any proposition *p*, either *p* or its negation non-*p* is true in that world. But how can we decide whether "Vautrin has a cousin" and "Lady Macbeth has four children" are true or false in their respective fictional worlds? It does not help, some claim, to retort that "actual" worlds display the same incompleteness; we may well not know whether or not there is life on Mars, but at least in principle the answer exists and waits to be discovered. True, more complex situations in subatomic physics cannot be decided even in principle, but at least the indeterminacy that governs specific domains seems to obey definite constraints. In fiction, indeterminacy strikes at random.

Such indeterminacy may have trivial causes. Within the limits of a finite text, not everything can be said. Borges' book with infinitely many infinitely thin pages is an impossible dream; actual texts are only fragmentary representations of their *Magna Opera*. Some texts are irreversibly damaged: Marlowe's *Doctor Faustus*, Gogol's *Dead Souls*. Incompleteness may result from the rules of the genre or from the whim of the narrator. In French classical tragedy, the news that circulates between antagonistic camps is spread by a nameless agent, skillful, precise, impossible to identify. Modern unrealiable narrators willfully hold back information or contradict themselves in the most confusing manner. Many contemporary texts more or less closely related to avant-garde techniques develop around a central gap of knowledge; in the most interesting cases, the concealed facts do not just happen to be inaccessible; rather, they seem to be absent, inexistent, in a radical way. *L'Inquisitoire* by Robert Pinget, for instance, contrasts the extraordinary wealth of information provided by the old servant to the mysterious questioner, with a certain structural inability of the interrogation to focus on definite incidents. Kafka had already made use of this procedure in *The Trial*.

Such thematized, one could say *enacted,* incompleteness can be construed as a reflection on both the nature of fiction and the nature of the world. The radical gap is but one of the numerous devices modern and postmodern texts display in their eagerness to lay bare the properties of fiction. As for the nature of the world, it is nowadays commonplace that, as inhabitants of a tragically shattered universe, we should not expect high literature to produce anything but broken, opaque mirrors of an inscrutable reality. Avant-garde texts, *nouveaux romans,* postmodern fiction, all capture antimimetically the difficulty of perceiving, of making sense out of the world; their disquieting incompleteness follows from equally disquieting (albeit possibly different) qualities of our universe. At least such is the accepted view.

It may be so; radical incompleteness and indeterminacy may be so deeply entrenched in modernity and postmodernity that any attempt to dislodge them would fail. But the alternative view is equally defensible. If structural qualities occasionally do grow wild (incompleteness today, for instance, not unlike allegory in the late medieval literature or layers of meaning in baroque or mannerist poetry), these qualities need not remain out of control forever—cultural equilibrium obtains again after a while, marginalizing these highly revealing abnormalities.

Faced with the unavoidable incompleteness of fictional worlds, authors and cultures have the choice of maximizing or minimizing it. Cultures and periods enjoying a stable world view will tend to seek minimal incompleteness by adopting various strategies that may be classified into two ideal types: intensive and extensive. To an unbound universe, well-determined and knowable in all its details, will correspond a tendency to extend texts as far as possible, filling them with lifelike effects, as if the difference between incomplete fictional worlds and the actual universe were one of quantity, and the limitations of fictional texts were only of a practical order. Vast realist constructions and *romans-fleuves,* from Balzac to Zola, from Galsworthy to Martin du Gard, arise from confidence that incompleteness can be overcome in principle and minimized in practice. An alternative approach, more archaic and only occasionally employed by writers of fiction, consists in assuming the completeness of the universe, together with the existence of a divine Book that describes it in full. This Book being of finite dimensions, and the wisdom of its author infinite, all conceivable truths, the entire contents of the *Magnum*

*Opus,* have been inscribed therein since before the beginning of time. To find their trace, the reader has to study the Book over and over again, literally, symbolically, anagogically, deciphering endless layers of meaning, opening the finite texts to the workings of infinite interpretation. The Kabbalists felt free to permute the linguistic units of the Torah incessantly in order to show that the message of each passage unfolds without end. Other books underwent similar treatment, and with no less fervor. Occult, pythagoreic, and mystic interpretations were built around the *Divine Comedy* and *Don Quixote.*

By contrast, periods of transition and conflict tend to maximize the incompleteness of fictional worlds, which supposedly mirror corresponding features outside fiction. In such situations lurks the temptation to lift gradually all constraints on determinacy and to let incompleteness erode the very texture of fictional worlds. Modernism gladly gives in to this temptation. Other periods and, within our own, other trends search for alternative solutions. The sixteenth century, for instance, was confronted with a disquieting ontological revolution: the fading away of medieval cosmology, the rise of the open, infinite universe, the return of classical mythology showing that the Christian had reigned and died. All this could not but enhance apprehensions about the indeterminacy and incompleteness of the universe, which were soon to be echoed in the construction of fictional worlds. Interesting insights about this process may be derived from a comparative study of medieval and Renaissance dramatic techniques. High medieval drama, the mysteries, and passion plays referred to a warranted world, completely described in the reliable Book, by appeal to which the somewhat fragmentary aspect of these plays, attributable to constraints of performance, could be remedied. By contrast, the fragmentary structure of a Shakespearean play relates to entirely different principles. While in a mystery play the scenes could afford to be short and not well connected, since the biblical text provided a background that filled in all gaps, in *King Lear,* in *Macbeth,* or in *Antony and Cleopatra* the rapid montage, the quick shifts of perspective, the transient secondary lines of action, all induce a nontectonic tension between fragments, which support themselves, as it were, by their own dynamism, not unlike a baroque painting, without resting on a basic, more complete, validating groundtext.

In Marlowe's *Tamburlaine,* the dramatic maxims require that Tamburlaine be successful from the very first attempt in any kind of enterprise he undertakes and that·this rule be known to him. His superhuman dimensions break the world's limits wide open. A Saturnian member of the family of giants whose Bacchic branch comprises his contemporaries Gargantua and Pantagruel, Tamburlaine brings along with him an incongruous model of the universe, in sharp contrast to the ontological tranquility preceeding his arrival, by claiming to be in touch with the very foundations of the universe, with the sources of Order and Chance and with the supernatural realm.

I would call the family of heroes to which Tamburlaine belongs the *ontological founders*. Like all heroes, they arise in worlds torn apart by conflict; but while in most cases lesser figures are content to solve the disagreement and establish a new social contract along the lines of the old broken contact, ontological founders strive to modify the very basis of the world. Radically rejecting the frame of reference within which they were born, they carry with them a world project drastically different from the actual world. But their medicine for a troubled world is much too strong, and the resulting clash considerably exceeds the initial disequilibrium. Since they do not oppose compatible adversaries, there is no possible surprise in the solution of their exploits; prone to endless victory, like Tamburlaine, or endless defeat, like his failing counterpart Don Quixote, the principle of their operation consists in the monotonous conflict between the old order and the new. Relentlessly, Tamburlaine's monstrous will conquers new provinces; with equal steadfastness, Quixote is checked and defeated in every attempt to implement his frame of reference.

But, whether met with victory or defeat, these world projects suffer, by virtue of their very nature, from an incompleteness more troubling than the usual kind of fictional incompleteness. It is not the absence of details that makes the worlds of Quixote or Tamburlaine indeterminate, for one can think of texts more schematic than these that are less affected by indeterminacy. Also, in neither case is incompleteness a purely poetological feature, as in Shakespeare, Diderot, or in Romantic or modern texts, where the fragmentary character of the presentation induces, as suggested above, a self-supporting dynamic construction, independent of a more basic validating text. From a poetological point of view, *Tamburlaine* and *Don Quixote* are rather simple texts, respectful of chronology and careful not to omit anything of consequence. But their ontological founders do not dispense with a more basic text. Tamburlaine's actions do not stem from strategic choices; they are based on his world project, passages from which he often recites with dogmatic assurance. Likewise, Don Quixote constantly refers to the basic texts of chivalric novels, their physical destruction at the hands of the well-meant priest and barber notwithstanding. Fictional themselves, born outside the primary world of the novel *Quixote,* just as Tamburlaine's will to power originates outside the established world of feudal kings, these texts thematize what we may call the *incompleteness of utopia,* whose peculiarity consists in an irrepressible tendency to feed on worlds more actual than utopia itself. Tamburlaine's world project must encompass the entire universe, visible and invisible; no pragmatic obstacle is strong enough to prevent its expansion. With no less stubbornness, Don Quixote reads every event around him according to the basic text, without ever being discouraged by empirical proof that his system does not work. For, in a sense, it does work. The rules of language, the indeterminacy of reference and translation being what they are, Don Quixote succeeds perfectly well in the detailed construction of a coherent, if precarious and incomplete, world version. Utopia devours actuality in various ways: Tamburlaine annihilates his adversaries by military might, Quixote confounds his with his gentle semantic obstinacy.

But Tamburlaine also knows how to gain new allies by persuasion: "Forsake thy king, he asks Theridamas, "and do but join with me,/ And we will triumph all over the world" (I.ii.172–3). And as soon as he witnesses the rhetorical unfolding of utopia, Theridamas decides to follow Tamburlaine. Not that he would have been offered the slightest proof of the verisimilitude of Tamburlaine's claims; the message he receives is purely symbolic. To use an expression favored by anthropologists, Theridamas is sensitive to "condensed symbols." These are economical and well-articulated systems of signs to be found in magically oriented societies, so that, according to Mary Douglas, "it is enough to strike one chord to recognize that the orchestration is on a cosmic scale. For Christian examples of condensed symbols, consider the sacraments, particularly the Eucharist and the Chrisms. They condense an immensely wide range of reference summarized in a series of statements loosely articulated to one another" (1973, p. 29).

In Marlowe's play, Tamburlaine's power is such a symbol: its magical quality casts a spell on its spectators (Zenocrate, Theridamas); it also needs the flowery rhetoric of Tamburlaine's set speeches to establish a cosmic framework that gives the symbol its resonance. On one side, the Fates, Fortune, Jove, and the entire mythology bring the heavens into the picture; on the other, geographical allusions to Egypt, to Christian merchants, Russian ships, the Caspian Sea, project the symbol onto the known earth. But, if so, the seduction of

Theridamas corresponds to some extent to the anthropological description of ritualism, as signifying "heightened appreciation of symbolic action," manifested in two ways: "belief in the efficacy of instituted signs, sensitivity to condensed symbols" (Douglas, p. 26). Theridamas' conversion indeed takes place in a highly ritualistic setting. The incompleteness of utopia is compensated for by the overwhelming richness of symbolic action, represented here by the rapturous rhetoric of Tamburlaine. The utopian project derives its radiant coherence from the condensed symbol, Tamburlaine's sacramental power, magically related to the heavens and earth. However, in utopian contexts we do not find belief in the force of instituted signs: by definition, utopian rituals lack the inner stability of time-honored rites. Thus much accent will be placed on *ritual emotions,* triggered by utopian speeches, rather than on the ritual action prescribed by tradition. The follower will have to display total availablity to the new world project, rather than formalistic fulfillment of inherited rules. This is not to say that utopian projects do not need a sacramental component: but since utopia is not a celebration of permanence but implementation of new worlds, the unfolding of the project will tend to ritualize the destruction of the old order. Against common wisdom, against traditional narrative structure and gratification psychology, Tamburlaine's cruelty increases with his success. The sacramental support of utopian advance consists in the ritual of Death.

Since we too live in a world of transition and conflict, the temptation arises to let indeterminacy take over our fictional worlds. Avantgarde strategies consist in fully assuming incompleteness and indeterminacy, and in pushing them to their extreme textual consequences. But this is not the only way left open to us and, as with the fictional strategies of Marlowe and Cervantes, contemporary writers have the option of building worlds that resist the radical workings of indeterminacy. In order to construct fictional systems accounting for the difficult ontological situations in which we find ourselves, we do not need to opt for maximizing incompleteness or indeterminacy. An important choice left to contemporary writers is to acknowledge gracefully the difficulty of making firm sense out of the world and still risk the invention of a completeness-determinacy myth.

This is the choice of Michel Tournier in *Le Roi des Aulnes* (The Ogre), the story of a Parisian garage owner who, under the cover of a trivial existence, stays in touch with cosmic forces of a yet unseen kind. Abel Tiffauges is a metaphorical ogre who receives his powers from a deceased friend and protector, also an ogre. He exerts the most extraordinary and unsuspected influence on the world: by a simple act of will he triggers the Second World War, during which, as a soldier and later as a prisoner of the Germans, he explores his own abysmal ambiguity. By vocation a carrier of beings, having Saint Christopher as his patron, Abel is capable of a demonic inversion of signs, an inversion that transforms him into a stealer of beings, an Erlkönig in the service of a German military school. At the end, however, the wheel spins once again; the last inversion of signs turns him into a beneficial carrier of people. He meets with death while fleeing the military school, carrying on his shoulders a Jewish child whose life he attempts to save.

All the elements seen in *Tamburlaine* and *Don Quixote* are to be found here: the shattered world, the private myth coextensive with the actual world and offering an unexpected, unacceptable reading of it, the extraordinary powers of the hero, the condensed symbol, the sensitivity to symbolic action, the new rituals based on emotion (called *phory* by Tiffauges). Has Michel Tournier been influenced by Marlowe or Cervantes? Spurious question: in an epoch that is as troubled as the Renaissance, he may well have rediscovered the way from incomplete worlds to ritual emotions.

# 5 ⸺Conventions

THE THRUST of my earlier arguments was directed against those segregationist practices that draw, in the name of philosophical realism, rigorous lines between fiction and nonfictional statements. Conventionalism has been encountered only briefly, but its rejection of referential approaches in the theory of fiction is as noteworthy as that mounted by realist trends (though it stems from different concerns and leads to differnt results). Its most radical manifestation can be found in the structuralist doctrine, but it also can be met in non-structuralist contexts.[1] Literary texts, under a structuralist-conventionalist view, cannot be taken to speak about states of affairs outside themselves, since any such apparent referring is regulated by rigid conventions that make those states of affairs behave like effects of a perfectly arbitrary illusionistic game. It would not make much sense to examine the structure of fictional worlds, nor the interplay between these and actual worlds; reality in fiction is just a textual convention, not so different from the compositional conventions of the rhyme pattern in sonnets, the five acts in tragedies, or the alternation between main and secondary plots in Renaissance drama and eighteenth-century epistolary novels. The literary trend that strove most conscientiously toward minute referential adequacy, realism, has repeatedly been described as a mere ensemble of discursive and textual conventions. And since language and discourse cannot copy reality, the realist convention is just as arbitrary and nonreferential as any other.

A claim like this rests on an implicit notion of semiotic convention that includes the traits of arbitrariness, obligatoriness, and unconscious character. In the continental semiotic tradition, these features can be traced back to Ferdinand de Saussure's theory of the linguistic sign. According to this theory, the phonetic side of the linguistic sign (the signifier) and its semantic content (the signified) are linked together by an arbitrary connection: the sound *tri:* does not relate to the concept "tree" by virture of any inner casuality; in addition, the meaning "tree" should be distinguished from the object tree. Prima facie, this stand seems innocuous, since the conventionality of the bond between sound and meaning as well as the distinction between concept and object have been accepted ever since Aristotle's philosophy of language. The novelty of the Saussurean approach consists in the synthesis between a classical conventionalist thesis and the romantic Humboldtian conception that sees language as a field of energy expressing the world view of the speech community. The classical component guarantees the formal organization of the semantic content of a language into an arbitrary yet systematic network of oppositions that remains independent from the world of objects by virtue of the distinction between object and concept. In accordance with the romantic component, the formal network projects itself into the world and organizes it in conformity with the linguistic a priori. In the act of naming a tree *tree,* we do not merely apply the appropriate linguistic label to an object, as common sense wants it; rather we isolate the object tree in the natural continuum only in as much as the sign *tree,* whose signified belongs to a chain of formal oppositions, forces us to do so.[2]

The Saussurean synthesis was further developed by Hjelmslev, who proposed a universal distinction in natural languages between the expression plane (the phonetic level) and the content plane (the semantic side), each of these planes being in turn constituted of form (the structural principle) and substance (the phonetic and, respectively, the semantic matter, as organized by form).[3] In each natural language the form of expression and the form of content arrange and systematize two amorphous *purports:* the phonetic continuum at the level of expression and the universe at the level of content; these, Hjelmslev adds, do not enjoy any kind of semiotic existence outside the form that raises them to the status of substance. The two forms, expression and content, each carrying along its correlative substance, adhere to one another in an arbitrary solidarity called *semiosis.* Since, moreover, in the Saussurean tradition oppostion is the main principle of form organization, the universe amounts to an amorphous purport organized into a substance by a linguistic network of oppositions. The shape of the language-bound network obeys only its internal logic; hence its arbitrary and conventional character. This network is unconscious as well, since we are deceived by the mechanism, do not perceive its functioning, but believe instead in nature's independence from language.

Hjelmslev's four-term structure has since been widely applied to various systems of signs, literary texts included. From a semiotic perspective, various forms of content obey only their internal op-positional logic, imposing it on the purport in order to structure it as the substance of the content. In simpler terms, autonomous se-miotic principles variously organize the world, rendering any notion of reference, representation, or adequacy to the reality ornamental, if not superfluous. Seen as governed by semiotic conventions, literary texts do not describe real or fictional worlds, but merely manipulate an amorphous purport on which they impose their arbitrary rule. Mythic and realist discourse are equally conventional and unmoti-vated; Balzac's novels do not resemble reality any more than do chivalry novels; they just make use of a different semiotics, as con-ventional and artificial as any.[4]

This argument, and along with it a widespread practice of textual analysis, rests on two theoretical moves: it entails first a definition of conventions as systems arbitrary with regard to the domain they govern; second, it assumes that semantic structures are born in some prior unexplained way, independent of the field of reference that they entirely determine. Severe conventionalism, combined with linguistic apriorism, repels empirical doubts and, since semiotic systems *con-stitute* reality, no empirical evaluation of the argument would ever be possible.

It is perhaps interesting to notice that while the semiotic trends chose the conventionalist path of development, the debate inside lin-guistics itself took a different turn. Contemporary linguistics has grad-ually abandoned its earlier apriorism and conventionalism, and shifted its attention from semiosis—the arbitrary link between meaning and sound—to language universals, innate grammars, and the links to cognitive psychology.[5] This shift has failed to make itself felt in literary theory. Still it indicates the difficulties experienced by the conven-tionalist approach in one of its traditional strongholds, the theory of language.

## Classical Conventionalism

If by convention one understands "an agreement between persons, nations; general agreement on the usages and practices of social life; a customary practice, rule, method, etc." (*Webster's New World Dic-*

*tionary,* 1970), traditional thinking about literature perennially has hesitated between conventionalist and nonconventionalist stands. The theoreticians of classicism believed that literature obeys a set of rules, but these rules mirrored the order of nature, be it through norms established by the ancients or through direct observation of nature by the moderns.[6] In spite of their acute awareness of literature's dependence on norms, the classicists did not develop an autonomous theory of convention; since literary norms did not differ from the laws of nature, literary practices different from theirs were simply discarded as erroneous. It was only with the advent of romanticism, when classicist rules began to be felt as artificial, that a theory of literary conventions developed which condemned conventions as exterior, fallacious norms preventing nature from speaking in its own voice. Closer to us, Russian formalism rejected convention again, on grounds not all that different from romantic historicism. The notion of defamiliarization is designed to contrast the new artistic work with the established literary conventions of a given historical moment: a good writer renders strange familiar objects and situations by presenting them from an unexpected angle, and breaking with the accepted perceptual and cognitive conventions.

But the classicist idea of literature as obeying a definite set of textual norms has not failed to make new appearances; and some of our century's theorists, notably T. S. Eliot, E. R. Curtius, and Michael Riffaterre, make claims surprisingly similar to those of the seventeenth-century partisans of the ancients. Eliot's statements about the synchronic nature of world literature amount to a variation on a classicist theme; textual interdependence is precisely what partisans of the ancients emphasized, as opposed to the veleities toward textual independence showed by the moderns. The stress on textual interdependence may lead to undervaluing referential power and to concentrating instead on texts and their formal properties. Devotion to the ancients reveals a strong attachment to ornament and decorum: Eliot believed that poetry is essentially music, of sound or ideas; its social function consists in keeping language alive. But since the music of poetry is a music of ideas, ideas in poetry are there mainly in order to make music. And, if the social function of poetry is to keep language fresh, the efforts of poetry should be linguistically oriented.

Also related to the ancients is Curtius' description of European literature as a texture of topoi that travel from one period to another and from one text to another, independent of historical determinations. A given literary text provides for a meeting place of recurrent themes and figures deriving in most cases from the classical age. While Eliot's antimodern maneuver evacuates referential strength by replacing ideas with music and language, Curtius achieves a similar result by reducing texts to their lowest common denominator: the commonplace.

In Riffaterre's intertextual theory of poetry, the poetics of Aristotle meets Saussurean semiotics in a most remarkable synthesis: Riffaterre denounces what he calls "the referential fallacy" by suggesting that, just as victims of the intentional fallacy mistake the authors for the text, the new fallacy causes critics to substitute reality for the representation thereof. In everyday language, words appear to refer vertically to the objects they represent, but in literature, in which the meaningful unit is the entire text and not the isolated word, lexical elements lose their vertical semantic force and act upon one another contextually, producing a new effect of meaning, *significance*. Significance differs from dictionary meaning; it is generated and governed by the properties of the text, by the ambiguities and the overdeterminations of the poetic language. The naive referential view, Riffaterre claims, fails to account for poetic effects, since the mechanisms of the latter involve constant reference to other words and texts. But this is the only referential link of literary works: self-sufficient, poetic texts do not speak about the world, they only refer to other texts. Dependence on the texts of other writers blends, in Riffaterre's theory, with semiotic rejection of the real world's referential autonomy. Classicist confidence that the ancients once and for all captured the rules of nature in their texts is lost; in its stead we are offered a Saussurean view that separates the semiotic systems from their unattainable referents, replacing poetic worlds by ever-changing conventions of intertextuality.

## Hume-Lewisian versus Saussurean Conventions

That language has conventional aspects has long been accepted as one of the familiar philosophical verities, periodically called into question by some restless thinker but soon reinstated as unquestionably valid. In a relatively recent occurence of this vacillation, W. V. Quine (1936) has argued that since the term *convention* entails the notion of conscious contract, linguistic conventions could not possibly have been established by overt agreement, for such an agreement must presuppose some form of already existent language. The development of language must rather have proceeded by slow evolution, trial and error, leading to the behavioral conglomerate we all know and which in no accepted sense of the term resembles conventions. Leaving aside unwarranted assumptions about conscious contracts, Quine argues, we should limit ourselves to the study of linguistic regularities. Language does not belong to the family of conventions, but to that of customs; and about these the only appropriate response is careful observation.

As a response to Quine's position, David Lewis proposed an analysis of conventions that includes nonexplicit contracts. Lewis' position comes close to Hume's definition of convention as "a general sense of common interest, which sense all the members of the society express to one another, and which induces them to regulate their conduct by certain rules." As the ensuing lines suggest, Hume does not assume that the expression of the common interest must be explicitly linguistic, though it can occasionally take such a form. The crucial element in Hume's account is that conventions do not derive their validity from explicit promises but from reference to the actions of others:

> I observe that it will be to my interest to leave another in the possession of his goods, provided he will act in the same manner with regard to me. When this common sense of interest is mutually expressed and is known to both, it produces a suitable resolution and behaviour. And this may properly enough be called a convention or agreement betwixt us, though without the interposition of a promise; since the actions of each of us have a reference to those of the other, and are performed upon the suppostion that something is to be performed on the other part.  (*A Treatise of Human Nature*, III.ii.2).

In Lewis' account of convention, reference to the actions of other people is modeled on coordination behavior and games. Two of his examples indicate the kind of gentle attention to the acts of others that the theory assumes to underlie conventional behavior:

> (1) Suppose you and I are rowing a boat together. If we row in rhythm, the boat goes smoothly forward; otherwise the boat goes slowly and erratically . . . We are always choosing whether to row faster or slower; it matters little to either of us at what rate we row, provided we row in rhythm. So each is constantly adjusting his rate to match the rate he expects the other to maintain.
>
> (2) Suppose several of us have been invited to a party. It matters little to anyone how he dresses. But he would be embarrassed if the others dressed alike and he dressed differently . . . So each must dress according to his expectations about the way the other will dress: in a tuxedo if the others will wear tuxedoes, in a clown suit if the

others will wear clown suits (and in what he pleases if the others will dress in different ways). (1969, pp. 5–6)

Although expressed agreement is often the basis of coordination, Lewis stresses the frequent absence of explicit communication in co-ordination behavior and games. If the problem posed by the situation is familiar, the solution will be tacitly found on the basis of precedent, but even in the case of new problems sophisticated subjects may solve them without communicating, and achieve coordination in accor-dance with the criterion of conspicuous novelty or saliency: in order for the other subjects to notice and expect each other to notice it, the solution has to be strikingly unique.

The definition of convention generalizes the analysis of coordina-tion problems. In solving such problems we learn how to handle future coordination situations, each precedent contributing to our ability to address new coordination problems. Extrapolation of past successes leads in turn to "the general belief, unrestricted as to time, that members of a certain population conform to a certain regularity in a certain kind of recurring coordination problem" (p. 41); the experience of general conformity leads to the expectation of it, which reinforces the conformity, since all members of the group have similar expectations. The group reaches thus "a metastable self-perpetuating system of preferences, expectations, and actions capable of persisting indefinitely." This phenomenon Lewis calls convention, whose def-inition will include a regularity in behavior, a system of mutual ex-pectations, and a system of preferences, all of which must be common knowledge within the population:

> A regularity R in the behaviour of members of a population P when they are agents in a recurrent situation S is a convention if and only if it is true that, and it is common knowledge in P that, in any instance of S among members of P,
> (1) everyone conforms to R;
> (2) everyone expects everyone else to conform to R;
> (3) everyone prefers to conform to R on condition that the others do, since S is a coordination problem and uniform conformity to R is a coordination equilibrium in S.   (p. 58)

In the light of this definition, the horizon of expectations within which writers and their public operate can be seen as the background of various coordination games involving tacit cooperation between the members of the literary community. The author and the reader must understand each other and be able to coordinate their moves in a fashion not too different from that of the two people rowing a boat in Hume's and Lewis' examples. And just as expressed agreement is not necessary for the implementation of an equilibrium of coordination, one does not need the actual presence of the other participant(s) in the game in order to reach the desirable conclusion. One can imagine a coordination game—finding a hidden object, a letter or a treasure—in which the participants are not allowed to come in touch with one another and must decipher signs left behind by the coplayers. Is the absence of the other participants an insuperable obstacle to finding the letter or the treasure and, consequently, to the obtaining of equilibrium? To further dramatize the question, is the death of one participant an obstacle? In Poe's "The Gold-Bug" the treasure is found in spite of Kidd's death: the game of conspicuous novelty succeeds across generations. Absence does not necessarily affect the game, nor does the game require absence.

The Hume-Lewisian perspective leads to conclusions opposed to those developed within a Saussurean paradigm. Games in writing are but a particular type of coordination problem, even though, based on Saussure's doctrine of the differential character of any linguistic system, Jacques Derrida has argued that linguistic exchange, even in an oral form, bears the mark of what could be called "primordial" writing. The Saussurean doctrine, as expressed by Derrida, assumes that every linguistic sign is but a trace of the absence of all other signs. Since this is an important feature of alphabetical writing systems, wherein the optimal differentiation between signs requires that no sign possess its own features but that these be economically distributed throughout the system, Derrida concludes that spoken language is structured like writing. Still a sign also points to the absence of the object it stands for: the sign "I" functions in the absence of the signified ego, as if it were an inscription of its death. Again, this is a feature of writing systems, whose operation does not require the signatory to be alive. Hence, Derrida argues, speech allows, even presupposes, the death of the subject: like writing, speech excludes the presence of the living voice from its act (1967a, "Supplement of Origin")

The above definition of convention might, however, help counter to some extent the philosophical portentousness of the death of the subject. Modeled as a coordination game, linguistic exchange can sometimes dispense with the copresence of the participants. Since coordination can be achieved in spite of absence, the death of one or more participants does not create insuperable obstacles for the game.

Therefore, absence does not have to be elevated to the rank of a pardigmatic rule of linguistic coordination. It offers only an example of a coordination game in which, depending on the purpose of the coordination, the participants put a special emphasis either on the unexpectedness of the clues or on their familiar character. The transmission of traditions, beliefs, rites, or texts across generations depends on strategies of stability involving the use of iterability as a source of mutual expectations; the establishment of new artistic trends, realism among others, calls for strategies of novelty, based on conspicuousness as a key to equilibrium. In religion, the two types of strategies lead respectively to ritualistic systems and mysteries; in social behavior, to sophisticated politeness versus casualness; in education, to repetitious versus problem-solving methods; in poetry, to formulaic versus innovative patterns. Formulaic literature, as analyzed by Milman Parry, Albert Lord, and Paul Zumthor, functions by virtue of the assumption that poems closely respect a set of preestablished formulas, known to both the poet and his public. Encoding and decoding Homeric poems, Serbo-Croatian folk narratives, or the poetry of the troubadours proceeds via reference to familiar schemata, as sources of mutual expectations.

The un-Saussurean perspective of the Hume-Lewis approach extends to the normative and unconscious aspects of conventions. Those who assume social conventions to be governed by a languagelike system are inclined to stress their obligatoriness and unconscious character; since in the Saussurean paradigm linguistic structure formally organizes our understanding of the world, there is no possiblity of avoiding its constraints, nor can we render it transparent to the intuitions of the native speaker. A most severe conception of artistic and literary conventions ensues: their obligatoriness and secrecy is such that literary texts appear to be woven by an invisible conventional hand in the absence of the author, whose disappearance Barthes celebrated (1968a). Conversely, in a Lewisian world, where conventions are stabilizations of coordination games, they are obligatory only in a weak, de facto sense; that brides at some periods in history dress in white is obligatory (when it is), only because this particular solution tends to become stabilized; other solutions remain possible, however. Likewise, in systems based on novel solutions, literary games change incessantly: the mobility of artistic conventions suggests their weak obligatoriness. This entails a considerable amount of choice, hence the need for awareness and deliberation: the irremediably unconscious aspect of Saussurean conventions is therefore inadequate.

True, in Lewis' definition a convention becomes such only when the community forgets to deliberate about its appropriateness. But the memories of its implementation can easily be recalled and the same game, or a modified one, can start again, leading to new solutions and new conventions.

## Conventions of Fiction

The literary theorist who comes closest to Lewis's sense of freedom and contingency is Barbara Herrnstein Smith, who has described a set of principles of cooperation followed by readers of fictional discourse.[7] By virtue of the *convention of fictionality*, literary utterances are perceived as representations of linguistic structures, representations that generate their own semantic context. This convention regulates the behavior of the readers by requiring from them a maximal participation oriented toward the optimal exploitation of textual resources. The convention of fictionality warns the readers that usual referential mechanisms are for the most part suspended and that, for the understanding of the literary text, outside data mean less than in everyday situations; so every bit of textual information must be carefully examined and stored.

I would add that Herrnstein Smith's convention functions as a more general constraint on reading and interpretation: maximal decoding is required of readers of history as well, especially when dealing with remote periods. The very popularity of history and biography indicates that many readers who are prepared to cooperate with the narrative-descriptive text also desire genuine historical information in return. On the other hand, archaic formulaic works, which usually presuppose a heavy battery of known prescriptions, do not direct the attention of their readers toward the same kind of effects as a modern text: reading strategies based on precedent differ from those searching for novelty, and it may well be that this distinction cuts across the conventions of fictionality.

A further important distinction entailed by a Lewisian approach sets apart *conventions proper,* which are stable, well-entrenched patterns of solutions to problems of cooperation, from *social games of coordination* that require cooperative solutions but do not necessarily lead to their entrenchment as conventions. In contrast, the semiotic approach tends to assume that every regularity of semiotic behavior reflects a rule of the semiotic code. Roman Jakobson's poetic analyses, for instance, treat every detectable pattern in a given poem, be it accessible to the reader's attention or subliminal, as an expression of the poetic grammar that governs the text in question. But the typology of literary convention needs to distinguish between *constitutive conventions,* which establish the very texture of the communicative process, and mere coordination regularities, or *pre-conventions.* A taxonomy of literary conventions that takes this distinction into account would find at least four quite diverse kinds thereof.

First, constitutive conventions set the main rules of social activities: in natural languages, grammar assumes this role; in a football game, the rules according to which it is played. The existence of these rules in the literary exchange is subject to doubt, and many writers deny that art can fruitfully be compared to language. But supposing that literary activity, though not a language *stricto sensu,* can be conceived as a complex coordination game, there certainly are numerous constraints outside which the game could not take place. Entrenched coordination equilibria, such as metrics, the form of a sonnet, the five-act division of a tragedy, appear to constitute the very frame whereupon literary exchange is meant to rest.

An example from metrics can be instructive. When reading or reciting the first of the two following lines:

> Not from the stars do I my judgement pluck;
> And yet methinks I have astronomy . . . (Shakespeare, sonnet 14)

we face several choices. Read like prose, the stressed syllables will probably be the following:

> Not from the stárs dó Í my júdgement plúck

A more theatrical reading can in addition stress the first syllable:

> Nót from the stárs dó Í my júdgement plúck

The sequence "do I," moreover, can be pronounced as "dó I" or "dó Í; an extra emphasis can be placed on "my," and, provided it leaves enough time between words, a highly emphatic reading could add a stress on "from":

> Nót fróm the stárs dó Í mý júdgement plúck

In spite of the diversity of possible scansions, after reciting the entire sonnet (and perhaps many more sonnets as well), one discovers several general regularities: for instance, the last but one syllable is virtually always unstressed or, more often than not, the even syllables are stressed, while the odd ones are more likely to remain unstressed. A tacit metric scheme takes shape, that of the iambic decasyllable—to which every competent reader of English poetry conforms and expects others to conform, since rhythm is a coordination problem and conformity to the metrical scheme provides the guidelines for the coordination equilibrium.[8]

Similarly, the efforts of modern narratology have been directed toward the discovery of the constitutive conventions of narratives. How do we know that a certain discourse or textual development is a narrative? In a similar way, the answer runs, to our mechanism for accepting that a certain sequence of words is a sentence, that is, by checking it against an internalized grammar. Narrative grammars contain information on narrators, the content of narratives, events and their organizations. Most of these elements can be seen as entrenched solutions, which by tacit agreement become constitutive conventions. Not unlike the fixed sonnet form, there are narrative patterns that require from the reader knowledge of the established conventions: first-person narrations, epistolary novels, or detective stories are recognized and enjoyed by virtue of an entrenched agreement whose cooperative nature makes it quite similar to Lewis' conventions.[9]

But not all predictable narrative effects qualify as conventions proper. A contemporary well-trained reader, as well as her nineteenth-century counterpart, knows quite well that large-sized novels published in England in the first half of that century most often deal with matrimonial questions, especially when the author is a woman and the tone is serious. In such novels, marriage will be actively sought as the optimal state of affairs for the protagonists, under certain social and sentimental constraints. A good reader knows that this regularity is part of the novel's background and that the right expectation makes the game possible. One understands what *Pride and Prejudice* and later *Jane Eyre* are about only when one expects, or realizes, that matrimony and the condition of women are central topics and that an intimate relationship links them to the novel as a literary form. However, such a regularity does not qualify as a proper convention, since uniform conformity to it does not obtain: not only do many nineteenth-century novels have nonmatrimonial topics, but those dealing with matrimony handle the subject in very diverse ways. The situation resembles coordination games, in which the strategies for cooperation are not yet ossified into conventions: each particular instance of the game, while sharing some of its features with other games, asks for specific skills and idiosyncratic solutions. Pre-conventions will thus include those literary regularities that do not reach the high uniformity of conventions and can therefore be understood as local rules or hints in a particular group of literary games. At the level of narration techniques, a similar situation arises in connection with, say, the embedded narrative (*Wuthering Heights*): in order to play the game well, one has to be aware of the romantic technique of embedding a story difficult to believe into a first-person narrative told by a reliable individual. That this awareness has to be learned is not an obstacle to the argument since, as with many games, we may start with a simple set of rules and gradually come to discover more and more complex strategies.

The distinction between naive and more sophisticated reading becomes essential, therefore. In a game-theory perspective, literary texts are assumed to be built around a few basic rules that give access to the text; while a naive reader knows these and only these rules, more advanced strategies can gradually become available through training and practice. Just as good chess players master not only the elementary rules of the game but are capable of applying such strategic laws as the principle of intermediary goals, or the principle of controlling the central squares, good readers know how to detect regularities that are invisible to less-trained readers. Advanced readers may know in advance the matrimonial outcome of *Jane Eyre* and enjoy the tortuous progress toward it, or they may have understood that Balzac's novels always turn on financial catastrophes, or that in *Remembrance of Things Past* virtually every character has an ambiguous sexuality. The Lewisian dichotomy between solutions based on precedent and those based on novelty can be applied to one and the same literary text, depending on the background of its readers. The embedding of a core narrative into a frame narrative can be perceived by a naive reader as a surprising innovation, whose rules and reasons he has to uncover by carefully observing clues planted by the author. A reader ignorant of this particular game does not know whether the first frame of *Wuthering Heights* is meant only as a transition toward a more substantial account or if it is destined to become the main thread of action, to which, after the presentation of the manuscript, the story will return. A more sophisticated reader, or the naive reader at a second reading, will replace the strategies of discovery by strategies of recognition. During a second (or sophisticated) reading, the transition from novelty solutions to solutions based on precedent helps to emphasize an important component of aesthetic pleasure, which the romantic and modernist traditions, with their insistence on spontaneity, innocence, innovation, and surprise, unfortunately neglect. Like all games in which skill improves with training, literary games enhance the pleasure of taking fewer and fewer risks, of feeling oneself more and more in control. As with the student of chess, the practicing reader senses the growing of his power and dexterity; he enjoys his progress and loves to continue the practice. So the abrupt romantic and formalist opposition of innovation to ossified convention should be modified to include the gradual assimilation of new games, the prolonged training of readers, and the progressive gain of control over new kinds of coordination problems.

To turn back to pre-conventions, it is not always easy to discern regularities that belong to the literary game from those engendered by the representation of social conventions established outside the literary exchange. That the ontology of revenge tragedies contains ghosts who often play a major role in the revelation of the crime *(Hamlet)* may be no more than a literary device—although it can be also argued that most of Shakespeare's contemporaries believed in ghosts. But the maxims of power in force in Renaissance tragedies ("An earthly crown is the most desirable thing," "Any limitation of supreme power is an adversary to that power") undoubtedly describe social beliefs and practices contemporaneous to the texts. In the Spanish theater of the Golden Age and in Corneille's tragedies, the code of honor respected by the characters is such that indeed each conforms to the code, each expects the others to conform to it, and each prefers to act according to the code, on the condition that the others do the same. But obviously the theatrical code of honor more or less faithfully represents a social convention in force in the aristocratic milieu contemporaneous to the play. To further complicate the situation, it must be noted that reference to social reality outside the text does not change the conventional status of the code inside the play, since a public belonging to a different period is perfectly capable of understanding *represented conventions,* even when these lack an effective social counterpart. Utopia and science fiction make us familiar with the technique of inventing nonexistent social conventions. Literary texts and myths, but also biographies, history, hagiography, often spell out conditions for social coordination.

Victor Turner has noted the interdependence between what he calls *social dramas,* which are spontaneous units of social process involving a crisis and its redress, and genres of cultural performance: "life, after all is as much an imitation of art as the reverse." Although the representation of social dramas lies at the origin of literary narratives, "some genres, particularly the epic, serve as paradigms which inform the action of important political leaders . . . giving them style, direction, and sometimes compelling them subliminally to follow in major public crises a certain course of action, thus emplotting their lives" (1980, p. 149). More generally, represented conventions often display a normative role: they operate as hints of the ideal behavior required from members of the community. Hence the strongly idealized appearance of some of these representations, both in classic and romantic literature. Conventions of courtship, for instance, as typified by *Astrée* or, more than a century later, by *Werther, The Elective Affinities,* and the prolific succession of romantic novellas and novels on the theme, concluding with the parodic *Tristan* of Thomas Mann, possess a distinctively normative ring; too severe to be faithful reproductions of social practices, these texts exerted nevertheless a lasting fascination on their public in the same fashion as the medieval lives of saints secured the attention of theirs: as models impossible to follow literally, but giving social behavior orientation and meaning.

Sometimes pre-conventions tacitly implement peculiar characteristics of the fictional world. Fifty years ago, in a strong rejection of psychological interpretations of Shakespeare's tragedies, E. E. Stoll described the "convention of the calumniator credited," which requires the good characters to believe the lies and calumnies of villains (1933, pp. 6–8). According to Stoll, since Othello's gullibility lacks a psychological basis, it can only be understood as an instantiation of the calumniator credited, like Glocester's credulity in *King Lear* or Arden's giving credit to his wife's confabulations in *Arden of Feversham*. It can be added that at the end of nineteenth century Ibsen's *Doll's House* was built upon a complementary variant of this convention, according to which innocents never manage to make themselves heard. Strindberg's *Father* thematizes the impossibility of not believing the calumniator, even when his or her malice is apparent. *The Dance of Death* by the same author is constructed around several kinds of calumny and gullibility. In Chekhov's *Cherry Orchard* the heroine lets herself be persuaded by the lies of a distant character, presumably wicked. Clearly, the rule of the calumniator credited, which in its generalized form requires the success of every deception, does not govern the literary behavior of the audience. Nor is it a represented convention, since the deceived character does not know about the rule and therefore does not conform to it willingly. But it is not a constitutive convention either, since the literary competence of the audience does not necessarily include it. A competent spectator who senses the rule of the calumniator credited will expect on the one hand that Othello believes Iago's insinuations but, on the other hand, as a witness of disloyal behavior, he will hope that the Moor does not trust the calumniator. In other words, this regularity occasions unusual expectations of a higher order that contradict the more current expectations. Yet new hypotheses and theories represent the regularities of the universe in an unexpected way; the content of a theory increases proportionally with its unexpectedness. Regularities like the calumniator credited do not proceed otherwise: to show consistently the success of deception is to submit that the world is governed by unexpected laws, or rather by laws that are surprising at one level but predictable at a higher level. Functioning as a set of *hypotheses* about the fictional world, this type of pre-convention constitutes an important part of the referential mechanisms of literature.[10]

### The Semantics of Tragedy

Semantic threads of this kind can be found in constitutive conventions as well: literary genres, for instance, often carry along strong hypotheses about their fictional worlds. These are less visible in the current definitions of genre, usually based on a mixture of criteria pertaining to the structural aspects of the literary text, its semantic characterization, and the conditions of its reception. The Aristotelian notion of tragedy includes the imitation of an action—a semantic notion; the change of fortune with its two components, reversal *(peripeteia)* and recognition *(anagnorisis),* which can be seen as a set of structural plot constraints. Catharsis, understood in a ritualistic framework or in a more modern psychological interpretation, refers to the process of reception.

A multiplicity of criteria leads to flexible definitions. In a classic paper (1956) Morris Weitz argued that aesthetic concepts have an open-textured quality; although their instantiations offer Wittgensteinian family resemblances, they stubbornly resist attempts to fix their definition once and for all. To "close" an aesthetic concept is ludicrous, Weitz maintained, since this would contradict the built-in potential for innovation that we feel to be a central characteristic of art.

Weitz's argument expresses in a strong way a familiar doctrine, often found in relativistic contexts: the orthodox historicist believes that cultural categories do not possess trans-historical essences because they depend for their definition on particular historical periods; similarly, the Whorfian anthropologist relativizes these notions to the cultural context in which they are used. But need the rejection of essentialist definitions lead us into severe relativism?

Let us assume for a moment that the meaning of aesthetic notions such as "art," "tragedy," or "portraiture," to use Weitz's own examples, may be represented in terms of their extension. The notion of art would thus be represented by the class A of individual works of art. The extension of tragedy would consist of the class T of individual tragedies. Weitz's argument rightly intimates that one cannot attach to these classes sets of properties shared by all potential members of the class. Indeed, if a set of universal properties existed, it would mean that every new object claiming to belong to the class in question would have to possess these properties. Such a requirement would closely resemble the position of neoclassical criticism, which embodied a narrowly circumscribed point of view. In contrast, the relativist proposal amounts to breaking up the sets of tragedies into mutually exclusive subsets historically or culturally indexed. Thus the set T of all tragedies would divide into, say, the sets $Tg$ of ancient Greek tragedies, $Tm$ of medieval tragedies, $Tr$ of Renaissance tragedies, $Tc$ of French classicist tragedies, and so on.

This extensional definition requires an ideal reader/spectator acquainted with all the tragedies ever written before an arbitrary date, say $t$, but who is unable or unwilling to formulate a clear definition of the genre. But does this reader/spectator know what a tragedy *is?* When presented with a certain text or performance, is he capable of giving the correct answer to the question: "Is this text or performance a tragedy?" Assume that the ideal reader/spectator has a perfect memory, that the texts/performances submitted for his judgment have been produced before the arbitrary date $t$, and that he is aware of this chronological detail. In order to decide whether a certain text/performance is a tragedy or not, all he has to do is check it against the set of tragedies he is acquainted with. If he recognizes the text/performance as one of the list, the answer is affirmative; if not, the text or performance is not a tragedy. If, however the text or performance has been produced after the date $t$, the case is undecidable, and according to Weitz the essentialist model is refuted.

Yet would a relativist model fare any better? We can imagine a set of ideal readers/spectators each acquainted with one of the sets of tragedies written before the arbitrary date $t$. Reader $Rg$ is acquainted with the set $Tg$ of Greek tragedies, reader $Rr$ with the set of $Tr$ or

Renaissance tragedies, and so on. A certain text (or performance) written before $t$ qualifies as a tragedy if at least one of these ideal readers recognizes it as belonging to the set of tragedies within his domain. Again, the decision is impossible for a text produced after $t$. The restrictions entailed by a relativist model are so strong that some of its consequences are clearly undesirable. One of the assumptions of the model is that the sets of tragedies $Tg$, $Tm$, or $Tr$ do not intersect: thus, each reader being acquainted with only one set, he cannot recognize as a tragedy a piece belonging to a different set. For instance, according to the model, the ideal reader acquainted with the French classical tragedies will not recognize as a tragedy Euripides' *Iphigenia in Tauris*, a highly counterintuitive conclusion. In the same vein, how would the model account for texts belonging to some set $Tj$ and which, as a consequence of a revival, Renaissance or Renascence, come to belong also to some other set $Ti$? More generally, how does the model account for trans-historical phenomena?

The committed historicist would certainly object to the proposed model as being oversimplified, even distorting: to represent historical periods in an extensional way as unqualified sets to which individual texts irreversibly do or do not belong is to miss the entire point. Cultural phenomena, he would argue, are subtle, fuzzy. A Wittgensteinian point in his favor would be that readers who have called "tragedy" various texts are as a matter of fact able to go on and guess which other texts are tragedies, without having grasped a property that all and only tragedies possess. Blunt extensional characterizations are bound to be false. But then how should we represent the fuzzy nature of cultural phenomena if not by using multiple criteria and flexible characterization? Genres are constitutive conventions, enjoying a relative stability but sensitive to historical movement as well. Some, like tragedy, are semantically homogeneous and posit strong hypotheses about fictional worlds. In such cases semantic criteria play a privileged role in the establishment of the convention. As we shall soon see, however, not even in such well-defined cases are semantic criteria the only ones that contribute to the definition of genre.

Semantically, tragedy can be characterized in contrast with mythical ontologies and epic sequences of events. Myths, being narratives, are composed of chains of events; by virtue of their privileged ontology, they serve as models of intelligibility for events in the profane world. The user does not need to question myths: it does not make much sense to ask, for instance, why Theseus abandons Ariadne and why Dionysius falls in love with her. For their users, myths do not need *explanada,* since as paradigms of sense they furnish explanations for profane events. That such-and-such a real-life woman has been abandoned by her lover and later marries someone else becomes intelligible in the light of Ariadne's myth. To be understood and justified, precarious existence needs the support of archetypical chains of events.

As long as the users strongly adhere to their myths, mythological religion offers a considerable advantage over other world views: non-mythological religions or scientific models, since it organizes the world in a remarkably detailed and durable way. As we have seen, when the adhesion to mythological constructions begins to weaken, the withdrawal of community support removes from myth its absolute truth, and what has been the very paradigm of reliability changes into fiction. But the ontological structure displayed by myths does not vanish; in particular, the hierarchic division of salient universes and the differentiation of the notion of existence remain essential features of the myths turned into fiction. Fictions speak of worlds that, without belonging to the real cosmos, use it as their foundation. Like the sacred universe, the world of fiction is separated from the real (or profane) world; the nature of the distance, however, has changed. While the sacred worlds enjoy a plenary reality that does not allow for questioning and needs no explanation, fictions dwindle to a secondary reality. Even if fictions continue to provide explanatory models for chains of events, the users of fiction can claim the right to assess their pertinence and appropriateness. One does not measure the truth of a myth; rather the truth of the world is measured against the myth. In constrast, one can evaluate tragedies; as the dramatic competitions in Greece show, one cannot avoid evaluating them. Hence the flexibility of fictions: explanatory models being constantly judged, fictions must struggle in order to have their truth recognized and accepted. Therefore fiction feels free to explore hypotheses, to construct models deliberately offered for public appreciation.

When adhesion to mythical systems declines, what suffers most is the intelligibility of events in the profane world. Formerly related to sacred events in a salient structure, human destiny tends to lose its explanatory principles once the mythical link weakens. From imitation of divine patterns, the sequences of human events turn into autonomous chains, which obey their own inner logic. Then it becomes necessary for the fictional activity to produce strong, striking sequences of events, in order for the weight of the fictional models to replace successfully the wornout mythical explanations. It is as if a mythical theory of the profane world had to be replaced by another theory or group of theories proposed by fictional works.

As shown by Claude Bremond (1973) in narratology and Georg von Wright (1966) in the logic of action, events obey a logic of possibility. Notably, the logic of epic poems develops according to a system of choices and decisions so that at every stage the protagonists enjoy a certain amount of control over their action. Clearly this is only an incomplete control, since the moves of other protagonists and the intentions of the gods constantly thwart the projects of each actor. However, the constraints on the freedom of the agents derive mostly from the strategic situation in force at each moment of the story, a situation determined by previous decisions and by the intentions and capabilities of the rival forces. In this respect epic poems represent a kind of "degree zero of the narrative," in which no constraint belonging to a higher level affects the concatenation of the actions.

In epic conflicts, the two parties ideally have the same chances of winning, and victory belongs in principle to the antagonist who uses more skillfully the rules of the strategic game. But, as critics have always known, in a tragic conflict the dice are loaded, most often from the very beginning: thus Agamemnon entering without hesitation into Clytemnestra's trap, Antigone fighting with her back to the wall against the authorities, Oedipus looking for a truth destined to destroy him. The nature of the deceit is often linked to the strategic configuration. Racine uses conflictual patterns in which one of the parties has no chance to win. In *Bajazet* the death sentence against the protagonists is sent to Byzantium before the beginning of the tragedy; in *Britannicus* the spectator witnesses the decrease in the fortunes of one group of antagonists (Britannicus and Agrippine); the tragic in *Bérénice* originates in the fact that Titus' decision is irrevocably made and remains unshaken.

Other means, only indirectly linked to the strategic configuration, can serve equally well as filters for possibilities, distorting the chances of the players. Shakespeare often stresses the strategic idiosyncrasies of the failing heroes: the way in which Hamlet, Macbeth, Lear, or Othello make their decisions cannot but radically weaken their chances of success, even if at the beginning of the conflicts they stand on a par with their opponents. Marlowe's tragic heroes, disposing of a matchless force, have the game distorted in their favor: thus the invincible Tamburlaine, the Jew of Malta, Doctor Faustus. Their fall originates in this incomparable force, which prevents them from correctly assessing the final strategic configuration. They end in disaster for having set themselves impossible goals.

Among other characteristic ways of limiting the chances of the heroes, one should mention heredity (Ibsen's *Ghosts*), the structure of personality (Strindberg's *Dance of Death*), the nature of the adversary (Beckett's *Waiting for Godot*). Perturbations in the structure of time often accompany the tragic distortion of chances: Barthes, for example, noticed the circularity of time in Racine's tragedies; other critics have commented on the structureless time in Beckett's plays.

More generally, the tragic protagonist has either no feasible choice of action or disposes only of an illusory choice: tragic plots thus suggest higher-order constraints on the chains of events, which eliminate a considerable number of strategic possibilities. Since the strength of an hypothesis is in proportion to the number of possibilities it excludes, the tragic hypothesis proves to be particularly strong. It presents the image of a universe in which the possible chains of actions are drastically limited: compactness and closure meet the tragic heroes.

But drastic limitation of strategic possibilities is not the only means of characterizing tragedies: like all literary genres, and more generally like any convention, tragedy is a self-regulating system. A local fault will be compensated by overdetermination in other areas. The compactness of the universe can be indicated by means other than the filtering of possibilities or the distortion of chance. With the usual outcome resulting in predicament or catastrophe, less skilled authors try to develop tragic themes the other way around, starting from the consequences. The plays of Webster or Tourneur overflow with poorly motivated murders, as if a certain saturation of catastrophes were an equivalent of the tragic hypothesis. Solutions miming tragic compactness sometimes employ the exterior features of the tragic tradition. The distortion of chances is better perceived at those social levels on which the characters can devote all their energies to the process of decision making: for a long time the use of this social level served as a substitute for the tragic proper. Corneille's *Le Cid* is called a tragedy mainly because the characters are kings and princes.

Nonetheless, in spite of its flexibility, tragedy seems to be losing its strength as a literary convention. The reason may be found, as with any weakening convention, in a displacement of the coordination problem: if my proposed characterization of the tragic hypothesis is correct, then it becomes apparent that proving the compactness of the world has been the main direction of the efforts made by philosophers, scientists, political thinkers, and even theologians. The tragic hypothesis enjoys such prestige, spreads with such celerity, that it is perhaps natural that dramatic works are no longer its privileged medium. Does this mean that tragedy is dead? Perhaps yes, in its original core, the tragic text; certainly not in the irresistible proliferation of its strategic hypothesis. This suggests that fictional hypotheses about the world are not forever confined within a given fictional genre. Since their circulation involves the entire cultural space, theory of fiction cannot be isolated from the general economy of the imaginary.

# 6 ⁓ The Economy of the Imaginary

MY FIRST chapters took issue with those philosophies of fiction that attempt to impose rigid limits on the phenomenon. At the same time, I argued against textualism in literary theory, the doctrine that reduces literary artifacts to their linguistic dimension, denying them reference to fictional worlds. I attempted to show that fictional texts employ the same referential and modal mechanisms as nonfictional uses of language, and that the logic of such texts is better understood when considered in relation to other cultural phenomena, in particular myths and religious beliefs. Various aspects of fictional worlds were then examined: borders, distance, size, incompleteness, conventionality; and in each case the flexibility of fictional worlds and their readiness to enter into the most diverse arrangements have been stressed. While proposing a general ontological framework for fiction—the salient structures—I argued that the demarcation between fiction and nonfiction is a variable element and that as an institution fiction cannot be attributed a set of constant properties, an essence. Thus my arguments should have conveyed an antiessentialist undertone, which was made explicit in the discussion of the definition of tragedy but which, I hope, was never too far from view. But reluctance to embrace an essentialist stand does not make the opposite choice, namely historicism, more appealing. The flexibility of fictional worlds does not entail their evolution according to the laws of history. Hegelian philosophy wants us to identify historical variation with teleological evolution. But is change always consistent with historical dialectics? Does it not instead often originate in structural shifts within paradigms, as structuralist thinkers have argued? Change may sometimes be attributed to external causes, such as the loss of belief in a well-organized mythology; sometimes to internal pressures, as with the rise of fantastic literature during the romantic era; sometimes just to the restlessness of taste, to the fickle moods of the Artworld. Moreover, it is far from assured that historical changes in one location on the map of the imaginary spread with sufficient rapidity and uniformity to count as genuine transformation. Older forms coexist with, and sometimes outlive, new adventures; we all still come into contact with folktales, mythological constructs, or the classics. Opinions and tastes are divided; depending on who is speaking, the nouveau roman is by now a forgotten anomaly, or the realist novel and its consistent characters have long since vanished. Alain Robbe-Grillet's novels have found a public in the last decade, but William Styron's have met with much more success, and while among his fellow nouveaux romanciers Robbe-Grillet is rather the exception, most of those on the opposite side maintain a good relationship with the public. To be sure, one can always dismiss philistine literature and commercial criteria; but, insofar as it fosters arbitrariness and parochialism, would not such a move be self-defeating? Moreover, the suggestion that the tensions between advanced trends and more traditional imaginary worlds is attributable to the peculiar wretchedness of our time does not withstand scrutiny. Other periods have experienced similar tensions, since the referential frameworks posited by literary fiction do not necessarily function by virtue of the ontological structure attributed to the actual world, and the ontologies of fiction enter into complex, conflictual relationships with the actual ones. The question thus arises whether it is possible to retain the notion of history of the imagination without either subscribing to a deterministic view of history or to an essentialist conception of fiction.

## Fictional Landscapes

Toward the end of the eighteenth century, a new cosmology was reasonably well established in the European scientific milieu, and was constantly conquering new social territories. Earlier, Fontenelle had described the pleasure and amazement with which a narrow French elite came into touch with the recent astronomy. Christian cosmology was far from dead, however. At the very end of the century, the unprecedented success of Haydn's oratorio *The Creation,* an enthusiastic celebration of the old cosmology, cannot be attributed simply to the beauty of the music. In defiance of the musical conventions of the period, *The Creation* relates the music to the libretto in an almost literal way. Should one think that the public was enjoying the oratorio despite its cosmology or because of it? At least some of the contemporary admirers of Haydn must have heard of the new theories about the planets moving around the sun; they must have been peripherally aware of an innovative cosmology while keeping their central commitments to an entirely different one, like a child who, at the age when it becomes more and more obvious that Santa Claus does not exist, still clings to her old beliefs while marginally sensing that her convictions may be obsolete.

This situation instantiates a remarkable property of ontological systems, namely the fact that they rarely command an unqualified loyalty. We saw earlier that, in salient structures, objects belong to two different sets of worlds and have different properties, functions, and ontological weight in each set. The worlds containing the individual called Jesus, the pole of the Kwakiutl worship house, or the grotto at Lourdes are clearly distinct from the worlds inhabited by the son of God, the Pole of the World, or the Holy Virgin. This is so not only for the skeptic and the materialist but also for the believer, who often perceives the world as profane in its texture, though sanctified by the epiphany of the holy that manifests itself precisely in these privileged, uncommon places, the holy spaces and beings that open channels between the two worlds. Sacred beings and objects, miraculous or prophetic grottos, holy mountains, places of worship, all these provide for the points of articulation at which the two worlds meet in what can be called a series of *ontological fusions*.

Fusions can conceivably be complete, in the sense that all the entities at the profane level play a role at the sacred level. Within the esoteric doctrines that teach universal symbolism, virtually every object belonging to the literal world has a place in the ontological framework of a secondary, symbolic world. The task of the wise is to decipher, for those objects perceived in the world of appearances, their place in the hidden, but all the more real, world. Pushed to their extreme consequences, all major religions contain projects of complete ontological fusion. Does not the presence of the holy convert the entire universe by attributing to each of its parts a religious meaning? Similarly, scientific projects are often based on complete fusions: atomic physics posits an invisible level of reality coextensive with the world of everyday experience but structurally different from it.

The manifestation of the sacred does not, however, always assume a pan-cosmic character. Most social organizations tend to limit the expansion of the sacred. When they succeed, the contact points between the two worlds are restricted to a well-defined set of elements:

the sacred spaces (temples, houses of worship, places of sacrifice), ritual objects, periods of celebration (ceremonies, feasts, festivals). The remaining space and time, the nonholy objects and activities, obey only the laws and constraints of the profane world.

Hence, the world view of a given community may divide into several *ontological landscapes*. European society at the end of the eighteenth century was still keeping the Christian element as an essential component of its ontological territory. This territory was, however, much wider than the Christian world: even among those not primarily interested in the progress of science, the rumor would circulate that new and disturbing cosmological theories were being proposed. We might safely assume that most of Haydn's admirers never managed to study the new cosmology closely. Yet any educated person could have planned to acquaint himself with the new system, the existence of which, together with a few of its general features, was common knowledge. In spite of the new territories, though, it was still possible to celebrate the beauty of the land that stood for centuries at the center of civilization: hence the enthusiasm with which Haydn's *Creation* was received. The oratorio must have been perceived as a magnificent opportunity to explore the old world, so beautiful, so close at hand, so reassuring.

Similarly, one may easily think of a population that, after having lived for a long time in the shadow of a great fortress, starts to spread out onto a much wider surface. The uninhabitable steep rock on which the founders had built their impregnable castle is declared a historic park and is used only as a tourist attraction. This does not prevent the castle from serving as a center and emblem for the expanding region: geocentric cosmology does not play a different role in our time.

Ontological landscapes foster the plurality of worlds; freedom of choice nonetheless appears to be subject to certain constraints, since most often people have a deep and stable feeling that they live in an ontologically coherent world.[1] If most societies seem to accommodate, or at least to authorize, some diversity in the ontological landscape, there still remain means to indicate that only one of these landscapes represents the world proper. Competition between neighboring landscapes always leads to a process of ontological focalization, to a sorting out and ordering of the worlds in place. The most conspicuous world model may then play the role of the absolute norm, of a high court that summons neighboring models for control and justification. In communities that adopt a central model, while still keeping other peripheral landscapes, the chosen model would serve as ultimate truth and regulating principle for the remaining versions: therefore, in case of conflict, the peripheral models have to yield. In typical European villages, for instance, popular beliefs more archaic than Christian cosmology, faith in local spirits, witchcraft, and such, coexisted with the new system for long periods. True, tolerance did not always mean freedom: accepted at the periphery, the slightest danger of expansion or conflict led to the exclusion of the archaic beliefs. If, then, orthodoxy imposes a dominant model, it is in order to protect a certain ontological focalization, a certain ordering of coexistent landscapes. For, observing the large number of beliefs and heresies condemned in the name of one set of convictions or another, one cannot avoid the impression that world models are in a continuous state of fermentation, change, and degradation—in a permanent movement against which the dogmatic reinforcement of a certain order may be the best defense. Thus rigidity of religious beliefs and more generally dogmatism of any sort could have their origin in the need for stability and for occasional normalization of the ontological landscape.

Such enforcement is obtained through a few recurrent patterns of landscape organization. Models that occupy the central area of the landscape may vary between two extremes: complete fusions versus flat literal universes. A complete fusion is a salient structure in which every element at one level plays a role at each other level as well (the converse need not be true). A flat or literal universe is a single-level construction, assumed to contain without residue all and only what there is. Fusions and literal universes may both in turn be strong or weak. A strong literal model is assumed to be the only faithful representation of all and only what there is, as happens in the case of early physicalism. A weak literal model may coexist with other weak literal versions or even with other fusions; thus a more tolerant philosophy of science accepts more than one literal representation of what there is; it can even accommodate, on occasion, nonliteral representations of the world.

At the other end of the spectrum, with strong fusions, the sacred world tends to cover the whole surface of the profane. In weak fusions, the two levels make contact with one another only selectively. The educated Christian at the end of the nineteenth century believed in a universe governed by natural laws; restricted to a few isolated points, the holy was surrounded by an entirely foreign texture. Religious philosophy solved this encirclement either by withdrawing into the existential moral field (since, according to this choice, the true place of the sacred is in the interiority of the subject) or by positing a sacred center of the world, unaffected by the progress of the profane. In both cases, in the heart of the literal we face the epiphany of a metaphor: the unseen donor of meaning.

At the margins of ontological landscapes, one finds leisure worlds, or worlds for pleasure, which often derive from older discarded models. Each culture has its ontological ruins, its historical parks, where the members of the community relax and contemplate their ontological relics. Greek and Roman gods performed this function till late in the history of European culture. Or marginal models may be used as training grounds for various tasks. Thus one of the functions of fiction is to cultivate abilities such as perceptual alertness, rapid induction, construction of hypotheses, positing of possible worlds, moral sophistication, linguistic proficiency, value awareness (as Eco, 1979, so convincingly argued).

The arrangement of ontological space strikingly resembles landscape architecture and urban planning. Strong fusions recall the use of the natural landscape by communities whose life is still close to nature. Weak fusions are not unlike nineteenth-century cities, where the inhabited space was clearly separated from green spaces, to the extent that citydwellers lived and breathed in different places. Strong literal models eliminate landscape variety, like the futuristic city from which the vegetable realm would have been excluded. Finally, weak literal models may be compared to our contemporary chaotic cities with their heterogeneous scattered neighborhoods, linked only by highway networks. For, like urban arrangements that render spatial coexistence of conflicting activities possible, ontological planning aims at avoiding or at least appeasing the inevitable clash between opposite world models. It rationalizes to some extent the variety of the ontological space; as a consequence, questions such as "Is proposition $p$ true or false?" can be referred to such and such an area of the general landscape. At the beginning of our century, a proposition like "Christ is a man-god," the truth of which unquestionably stood at the center of a strong medieval fusion, remains true within the space arranged for this kind of sentence, without being true everywhere in the ontological landscape—not unlike the activity of breathing fresh air, which at some point in human history was coextensive with most human activities but became restricted for the dwellers of the modern megalopolis. And like the social rules of behavior prescribing special leisure activities dedicated to the periodic consumption of fresh air, in complex ontological arrangements elaborate rules of etiquette indicate in detail which propositions should be granted in various contexts and situations. Propositions that are obviously true in church on Sunday are less so in different contexts, in say, professional meetings.[2]

Like any order, ontological planning may trigger hostile reactions: one quite serious cultural condition may be called ontological stress. Caused by difficulties of orientation among the complexities of modern ontological arrangements, this type of stress leads to the weakening of our adjustment to ontological landscapes. Its first victim was Don Quixote, unable to distinguish actuality from fiction. Since ontological distinctions have become much more subtle and complex, users of contemporary ontological arrangements must travel between heterogeneous if not plainly hostile landscapes to which they are expected to adjust rapidly and only for short periods of time, not unlike modern citydwellers who cross long distances between work and home. But our capability for ontological adaptation cannot tolerate more than a certain amount of change, and when the threshold is reached, it becomes difficult to avoid reactions.

Such reactions vary between nihilism and nostalgia. Nihilists interpret changes from one landscape to another as signaling the complete absence of order. To them, each landscape is only the deceitful ossification of one kind of illusion. To establish oneself somewhere, to dwell in a world model, is in the nihilist's eyes a mortal sin. Conversely, the nostalgic is homesick for old times when ontological stability was still the rule. Nostalgics of various persuasions, craving for the age of innocence, the age of cathedrals, Victorian order, Vienna at the turn of the century, are fascinated by the alleged simplicity of assent these periods required.[3]

Nihilism assumes that the simultaneous presence of several world models cancels the credibility of each model. Their multiplicity stands to prove that all are fictitious, and the choice between these fictions is made according to purely utilitarian criteria. Any version is good, if it serves a certain purpose; marginal or obsolete landscapes have the same right to attention as central versions; yet the centrality of the latter is only a question of convenience, or convention. In turn, by rejecting ontological multiplicity, nostalgics in their own way consider the surrounding ontologies as mere fictions, at least in comparison with the overthrown dogma.

I have just employed the term "fiction" as synonymous with error. Users of world models, however, spontaneously make distinctions between fiction and error, on the one hand, and fiction and truth on the other. They also know that world models can serve more than one series of users. A given model may lose the assent of its users without, however, being irrevocably discarded: deposed world versions often find secondary users. Mythologies, we have seen, survive this way. Nelson Goodman once suggested that we should replace the question "What is art?" by "When is art?" Also, one might simply be tempted to ask "When is fiction?" and offer a pragmatic answer: fiction is when world versions find secondary users.

But an answer of this kind would not cover all cases. For if fiction were only a special use of models produced elsewhere and later abandoned as obsolete, how could one explain the observation that most societies maintain some sort of nonreligious fictional activities, such as the "laughing stories" of the Cherokees, animal stories, anecdotes, folktales, and so on. To derive these from older unused or degraded myths is not always easy. On the contrary, a considerable number of folktales that are based on nonmythical material may have originated in the observation of current social life. They appear to have been designed independently of any other discarded world models.

Instead of defining fiction in historical terms only, as the result of decayed myth, we should perhaps characterize it as well in terms of ontological landscaping and planning. Taking the division of the ontological space into central and peripheral models as a very general formal organization of the beliefs of a community, we may localize fiction as a peripheral region used for ludic and instructional purposes. The concrete content of the marginal ontology would thus count less than its position within the functional organization; indeed, fictional space can accommodate almost any ontological construction. This would confirm the earlier contention that fiction is both a pragmatic and a semantic notion, since the organization of cosmological space obeys pragmatic reasons while the structure itself is clearly semantic. Also, the choice of the particular models that fill the fictional space has pragmatic undertones. Do these models originate in specially constructed versions? old discarded ones? actual models used fictionally for only a short while? But the regularities of the peripheral space itself possess semantic features.

## A Functionalist View of Fiction

Though they strive to include history as an important component, my suggestions are not historicist in the narrow sense of the term. They do not imply that history's course is in any way determined by material or cultural causes. Instead, the model suggests a less deterministic picture, one that resembles a strategic game, chess for instance, wherein the strategic configuration of each stage of the game depends simultaneously on the rules of the game, the configuration in force at earlier stages, and the particular strategic aims pursued, with more or less talent, by the participants.

Similarly, the economy of the imaginary must obey various general constraints, in all probability more flexible than those followed by strategic games. These might include cognitive and developmental restrictions, such as the *compositional constraint,* which requires non-empirical beings to be made up mostly of empirical components, or the *ordering constraint* according to which the development of the imagination follows irreversible (but not deterministic) sequences: complex forms presuppose simpler ones; drama develops from ritual while the converse is not true *(pace* Artaud); when myths become fiction they do so massively, through conversion of entire pantheons, while stories grow into myths one by one and in an unobtrusive fashion. The economy of the world models in use at a certain time depends on earlier stages, as centuries of research about such dependence have proven beyond doubt. But, again as in a strategic game, the economy of the imaginary also rests on systems of purposes and expectations that, within the historical horizon provided by the already existent solutions, delineate the new stage. Admittedly the notions of socio-cultural purpose and expectation are far from being transparent—but perhaps it is enough to mention them in order to call attention to the teleological aspect of cultural enterprises, and challenge our reluctance to handle final causes. And if entire cultures are too complex to have definable holistic purposes, at least fictional economy can be characterized as a functional system.[4]

It should be noted that a functionalist view of fiction does not entail the existence of explicit, unique, and constant purposes; nor does it suggest that there are stable means of achieving such purposes. Fiction pursues families of goals with uneven and ever-changing determination, switching emphasis from one aim to another, abandoning projects before completion, succeeding in secondary areas just when it fails in more important endeavors, obtaining by luck what had been denied to labor. Production of fiction bears the mark of instability; this may be attributed to the multiplicity of purposes, the multiplicity of structural means of achieving them, the lack of stable dependencies between structure and aims, or to all these factors combined.

Among the teleologic aspects of fictional activity, I would include the referential purposes of fiction. Reference in fiction rests on two fundamental principles that, while shared by fiction and other activities, have for a long time constituted the privileged core of the fictional order: the *principle of distance* and the *principle of relevance*. Creation of distance could well be assumed to be the most general aim of imaginary activity: the journey epitomizes the basic operation of the imagination, be it realized as dreams, ritual trance, poetic rapture, imaginary worlds, or merely the confrontation of the unusual and the memorable. Scandal, the unheard-of, the unbearable tensions of everyday social and personal life, are expelled from the intimacy of the collective experience and set up at a distance, clearly visible, their virulence exorcized by exposure to the public eye, by the safety net of exemplary distance. Sagas and epic poems offer the paradigms for the literary framing of real characters and happenings. The salient two-level structure that furnishes the semantic pattern to be extended to all fictions instantiates the same operation.

Symbolic distance is meant to heal wounds carved with equal strength by unbearable splendor and monstrosity in the social tissue. But the cure cannot work unless it is somehow shown to pertain to actuality. Symbolic distance must be complemented by a principle of relevance. Hence the proposition theory of artistic meaning, which, though open to criticism in its more punctillious versions, captures an important, ineliminable intuition, namely that literary artifacts often are not projected into fictional distance just to be neutrally beheld but that they vividly bear upon the beholder's world.[5] Their relevance does not have to be conceived according to a single model, be it that of logical entailment, conversational implicature, judicial decision, or ideological presupposition. These models have a subordinate status, insecurely linked to the encompassing, emergent role of relevance. Depending on various decisions and conventions, some may be overemphasized, others absent. Medieval exempla are constructed as generalizations: since $x$ who did mischief was so horribly punished, all $x$'s who do mischief shall share that fate. The venerable pattern, already noticeable in the most archaic folktales, valiantly survived through the vicissitudes of artistic evolution. It is not only Phaedra's misplaced love and its mythological punishment that impress us; *The Scarlet Letter, Anna Karenina,* the narrator's tragic infatuations in *Remembrance of Things Past,* or Sabato's *Tunnel* press the same point. And once the generalization is reached, a new conclusion gives these fictions vividness and appeal: since this can happen to anyone, it also can happen to *me.*

But the relevance of fiction does not limit itself to logical conclusions and moral generalizations. Fictional texts often interest their public merely by offering information on less familiar periods, regions, cultures, trades, or kinds of behavior. We do not read *Moby Dick* only to witness the hybris and tragic end of Captain Ahab, but also to learn about life on a whaling ship in the first half of the nineteenth century. With inexhaustible patience, the author strives to enlighten his public on whaling matters, and some of us get caught up in the long documentary passages, just as some of Balzac's readers enjoy the meticulousness of his descriptions. Most often, documentation is itself determined by the need for conspicuousness and scandal; this causes the unending flow of fictional texts on wars, holocausts, and exceptional tragedy in the life of ruling classes or outcasts.

Change in taste threatens entrenched solutions and favors diversity of procedures. Critics of contemporary culture have not failed to notice the trend toward a drastic reduction of fictional distance that brings fictional worlds as close as possible to the beholder. Frames and conventional borders seem to vanish, and the purpose becomes achievement of immediacy. The principle of relevance has been challenged too: many modern fictional texts playfully prevent the audience from reaching swift conclusions, moral or otherwise. Yet, since distance cannot be altogether abolished, the gap between us and the hyperrealist statues in contemporary parks will never be bridged. Henry James's or Kafka's ambiguities do not signal the end of relevance; at most they may indicate a transformation in the kind of relevance aimed at. Just as the tonal simplicity of Vivaldi's compositions is gradually replaced by more sophisticated procedures, culminating in the tonally equivocal systems of Wagner, Richard Strauss, and Mahler, simple inferential practices give way to richer literary systems, and inferential relevance (Lear's pride leads him to destruction) gradually leads to diffuse relevance (Kafka's *Castle* as an undetermined parable of the human condition).

Fictional worlds are the main repositories of structural features employed for referential purposes. They are, in most cases, related to the worlds of common sense, and bear the weight of ontological and epistemic assumptions, but they also reflect the technical sophistication of the author and his milieu and the different purposes that the construction is meant to achieve. Cosmologies, we saw, vary between salient, multilevel organizations and flat, literal ones. The more luxuriant worlds are closer kin to the wealth of early mythologies, while later fictional worlds bear a notable mark of austerity.

In historical societies we are perhaps entitled to see fiction as an institution destined to take over the place of myths and fairytales. In this sense, did not literary fiction begin as a truth project, meant to record memorable facts and to bring some credibility to the wilderness of myths? Yet the opposite tendency, rooted in fairytales, has not failed to take its revenge: the fantasy project deploys itself periodically, apparently meaning to break up the compactness of flat worlds and to bring back the kaleidoscopic opulence of less constrained imaginations. Romance versus epos and tragedy, fantastic literature versus realism, these were and still are cyclical fights between and two projects, with varying chances of temporary success according to the religious context (since naive religiosity tends to favor romance), to the social milieu (with idle groups preferring fantasy and compulsive ones inclining toward truth), to the level of saturation with the opposing project. Thus *Quixote* could have appealed to a period overfed with fantasy, whereas *The Master and Margarita* exploded in a context in which realism was the sternly enforced obligation.

Variation in ontological wealth is supplemented by epistemic principles. Again in opposition to early myths, fictional production brought along a technique of editing and rationalizing the sequence of events that resulted in well-balanced stories or plays, optimally focused on small groups of states of affairs. Compared with what we know about primitive myths, Greek myths included, everyday narratives, anecdotes, and folktales display a remarkable compositional unity and a maximal concentrating of interest on the narrative topic. But narrative discipline and compositional unity never had the power to impose themselves decisively upon fictional production. Just as the ontological severity of the truth project has periodically been mitigated by the intervention of fantasy worlds, the compositional severity of well-focused narration is periodically contradicted by dispersion, faulty arrangement, and incoherence, all eminently visible in primitive myths but reemerging in Greek novels, in chivalric novels, in the menippean and carnivalesque traditions, in many baroque and eighteenth-century novels, and again in our century in the modernist and postmodernist context.

Yet, in the end, all this restlessness appears quite well tempered, for every period, no matter how diverse and sophisticated its functional arrangements, seems to have at its command a certain number of indispensable elements. In almost every place and time we find a more or less complete thematic set, covering the main human concerns, social or existential. Birth, love, death, success and failure, authority and its loss, revolution and war, production and distribution of goods, social status and morality, the sacred and the profane, comic themes of inadequacy and isolation, compensatory fantasies, and so much more, are always present, from early myths and folktales to contemporary literature. Changes of taste or shifts of interest seem to affect the inventory only marginally. Since we need an alien space in which to deploy the energy of the imagination, there have always been and always will be distant fictional worlds—but we may also use close fictional worlds for mimetic purposes, in order to gather relevant information or just for the pleasure of recognition. Moreover, we find incoherent fictional worlds everywhere, worlds destined to provide a sense of dizziness and playful transgression. Distance, relevance, and dizziness, mixed in various proportions, give each period its peculiar flavor, but hardly ever is any of these components missing. Cultural arrangements may well attempt to stabilize these recurrent fictional components into durable consensual patterns; their perennial failure to arrest kaleidoscopic multiplicity allows the history of fiction to unfold. Yet this inevitable displacement incessantly brings forth the familiar elements, and history itself is but the surprising sway of colors radiated by the same few shiny splinters.

Notes

References

Index

# Notes

## 1. Beyond Structuralism

1. Woods (1974) examines in detail how fiction challenges various logical models. Routley (1979) believes that "literary phenomena rather convincingly show the inadequacy of most going formal semantics" (p. 3).

2. Searle (1975b) delineates a speech-act theory of fictional discourse, to be discussed in Chapter 2. Goodman's relaxed epistemology grants artistic fiction a dignified status (1978, 1984). See Elgin (1983) for a detailed discussion of Goodman's theory of reference.

3. The best presentations of the classical structuralist doctrine are Scholes (1974), Culler (1975), Chatman (1978), and Rimmon-Kenan (1983). Rimmon-Kenan's and Prince's (1982) books go beyond structuralist literary theory and include more recent ideas and material. Culler (1982) offers a thorough discussion of the relations between structuralism and poststructuralism. See also P. Lewis (1982) and the exchange between Hillis Miller (1980) and Rimmon-Kenan (1980). Godzich (1983) analyzes the American reception of Derrida's thought, while Martin (1983) discusses the historical background of poststructuralism in America.

4. Lévi-Strauss (1963), pp. 208–209. It should be noted in passing that the arbitrary character of linguistic signs has always been a commonplace of logic and philosophy of language. Saussure himself was aware of this when he wrote: "The principle of arbitrariness has never been contested by anyone" (1916, p. 68).

5. The most powerful philosophical statement against phonologism in anthropology is of course Derrida's chapter "The Violence of the Letter: From Lévi-Strauss to Rousseau" (1967b, p. 101–140). In Pavel (1979) I criticized the use of phonological models in myth analysis, basing my arguments on the constraints of classical phonology. In a recent book, Brooks (1984) criticizes structuralist narratology for its inability to represent the dynamism

and temporality of narratives. See also Graff (1979) and Margolis (1983), who vigorously attack structuralist and poststructuralist practices. Hartman (1980) and De Man (1983) offer meditations on the present state of literary studies; without rejecting structuralist contributions to literary theory, they plead in favor of a renewed literary hermenentics.

6. Ricoeur (1984), chap. 2, criticizes the semiotic constraints on narrativity. A detailed presentation of the narrativist/nonnarrativist controversy in contemporary theory of history can be found in Ricoeur (1982), part 2, secs. 1 and 2.

7. Barthes (1966), Todorov (1968, 1971), Genette (1972), and Bremond (1973) are of course the classics of the period. Genette (1983) answers his critics of the previous ten years, convincingly showing the viability of the best results of structuralist poetics.

8. In fact, Propp's first book (1928) served as a preliminary step for a historical study of the folktale (Propp, 1946). For a severe evaluation of Propp (1928), see Bremond and Verrier (1981).

9. To Lévi-Strauss's criticisms (1960), Propp (1966) opposes a remarkable yet little known answer.

10. For a recent presentation of the "semiotic square" see Greimas and Courtés (1982), pp. 308–311. Its applications to narrative analyses are criticized by Bremond (1982).

11. Kirk (1970) raises a similar point: "It seems to me, however, that the 'meaning' of the myth is to be found, not in any algebra of structural relationships, but quite explicitly in its *contents*" (p. 71).

12. Among recent discussions that have raised doubts regarding text closure, see Fish's radical criticism of textual autonomy (1982), but also the more moderate stands of Riffaterre (1978) and Genette (1982).

13. On the distinction between structural and aesthetic properties, see Sibley (1959), Walton (1970), Margolis (1977), and Pavel (1982, 1985a).

14. Notably in Chomsky (1957, 1965). Interestingly, the structuralists produced no real answer to Chomsky's criticisms.

15. On literary competence, see Culler (1975), pp. 113–130. Prince (1973, 1982) and Pavel (1976, 1985b) propose transformational-generative grammars of plot. Remarkable work on narrative structures and content has been pursued in the framework of artificial intelligence. See Schank and Abelson (1977), De Beaugrande (1980), Lebowitz (1984).

16. Notably Woods and Pavel (1979), Rieser (1982), issues 17 and 19–20 of *Versus,* and Csuri (1980).

17. Kripke's lecture at the University of Western Ontario (1972b) has provided the stimulus for my own research on fictionality. My arguments have been strongly influenced by Doležel (1976, 1979, 1980, 1983), Eco (1979), and Ryan (1981 and forthcoming). Equally essential to my argumentation are Danto's (1981) and Margolis' (1977, 1980) ontology of art, Putnam's (1960, 1970, 1975) functionalism, and Walton's (1978, 1984) theory

of fiction as a game of make-believe. The themes developed in these papers and books are so intimately woven into my text that I could not allude to them on each occasion. Hrushovski's (1979, 1984) ideas about fictionality are closely related to mine and often influenced my position. Rimmon-Kenan (1983) stresses the links between contemporary narrative poetics and the seminal work of Hrushovski and the Israeli school of poetics. I must also express my indebtedness to the luminous thought of Sora (1947, 1978); the ideas of his latter book are briefly presented in Pavel (1980).

## 2. Fictional Beings

1. Russell (1905b) presents his argument as a criticism of Frege (1892). Before 1905, Russell's ontology allowed for nonexistent individuals; see Cocchiarella (1982).

2. A theory of literature in terms of "pseudo-statements" based upon the emotive use of words has been developed in Ogden and Richards (1923) and Richards (1953). Its best known criticism can be found in Wimsatt and Beardsley (1949). See the discussion in Beardsley (1981), pp. 119–122.

3. Expressed in Strawson (1956, 1964). Russell (1957) briefly answered Strawson's argument from the point of view of the philosophy of mathematics.

4. Ryle (1933), published together with the paper of Moore (1933). Among more recent authors who argue against classical segregationism are Eaton (1972) and Blocker (1974). An important statement about segregationism is Rorty (1979).

5. Founded by Austin (1960) and developed by Searle (1969, 1975a, 1979), speech-act theory has influenced the theory of literary genres (Todorov, 1977), literary discourse (Pratt, 1977), and various poetic and dramatic analyses. An early survey and bibliography is to be found in Fanto (1978). Fish (1976) and Margolis (1979) strongly criticize some of these applications. Theories of fiction based on speech-act theory have been proposed by Gale (1972), Searle (1975b), and Gabriel (1979). Martínez-Bonati (1981) offers an insightful theory of fictional discourse based on a phenomenological approach; see the excellent discussion in Ryan (1984). Walton's criticism (1983a) of the speech-act theory of fiction reproaches Searle for the use of authorial intention in his definition of fiction. Walton argues that we can treat as fiction texts that were not conceived as such by their authors.

6. Price (1934–35), Malcolm (1951), Woozley (1952–53), and White (1957) have proposed conceptual analyses of knowledge and belief not yet influenced by the applications of formal modal semantics to epistemology.

7. On various occasions Putnam has insisted on the philosophical similarities between the deconstructionist opposition to logocentrism and Quine's views on the indeterminacy of reference; see, e.g., Putnam (1983, 1984). Ironically, Derrida's major statements against logocentrism in contemporary

philosophy (1967a, 1977a, 1977b) do not address the more rigorist views of, say, Frege, the early Wittgenstein, or Chomsky's naturalized Cartesianism, but precisely take issue with its more open-minded and tolerant varieties, from Husserl's phenomenology of logic to Austin's and Searle's speech-act analyses.

8. A resurgence of work on the topic of voice is signaled by studies such as Ong (1982) and Zumthor (1983), which include ample bibliographies on oral literature. Narrative voices have been the object of a long and rich tradition of research from Booth (1961) to Genette (1972), Cohn (1978), Banfield (1982), and many others.

9. In this apologue, we may recognize an updated version of Rotrou's poignant *Le Véritable Saint-Genest* (1647).

10. This story forms the object of the first few chapters in Benjamin Constant's *Adolphe*.

11. Meinong's article (1904), criticized by Russell (1905a), and other aspects of his theory are discussed by Findlay (1963). On nonempirical objects, see Chisholm (1973) and Lambert (1974, 1976). Routley (1980), Parsons (1980), and Lambert (1983) have proposed detailed Meinogian logics. The implications of Meinongian treatments for the logic of fiction are discussed critically by Van Inwagen (1977), Lewis (1978), and Woods (1982).

12. Howell (1979). An illuminating discussion of contemporary models in theory of fiction can be found in Ihwe and Rieser (1979), published in the same issue of *Poetics* as Howell's article.

13. The relevant texts are Putnam (1970, 1973, 1975), Kaplan (1968), Kripke (1972a), Donnellan (1966, 1974), and Linsky (1977). Schwartz (1977) collects several important papers on the topic, with an introduction and a good bibliography.

14. In a different context, fragment 688 of Pascal's *Pensées* dramatically contrasts identity and qualities: "what about a person who loves someone for the sake of her beauty; does he love *her*? No, for smallpox, which will destroy beauty without destroying the person, will put an end to his love for her. And if someone loves me for my judgment or my memory, do they love me? *me*, myself? No, for I could lose these qualities without losing my self." The abbreviation theory of proper names belongs to Searle (1958); the cluster theory, to be discussed shortly, is based on Wittgenstein (1953).

15. Tate's adaptation of *King Lear* can be read in Summers (1966).

16. Kripke (1979) defines the speaker's referent of a designator to be "that object which the speaker wishes to talk about, on a given occasion, and believes fulfills the conditions for being a semantic referent of the designator" (p. 15).

## 3. Salient Worlds

1. In a different philosophical context, fictionalist treatments have been applied from time to time to epistemological and cultural problems. Two typical examples are offered by Bentham's theory of fictions, republished by Ogden (1932), and Vaihinger's philosophy of "as if" (1911).

2. Kripke (1959); an alternative treatment can be found in Hintikka (1963). Loux (1969) collects several important papers in the metaphysics of modality.

3. D. Lewis (1970) and (1973), pp. 84–91; see also Loux (1979), introduction, pp. 46–48.

4. Plantinga (1976), Stalnaker (1976); also Rescher (1973).

5. Winner (1982) makes use of the metaphor; Prince (1983) also argues in its favor. Wolterstorff (1980) constructs an encompassing theory of art in terms of fictional worlds. Phenomenologist philosophers like Ingarden (1965) use a terminology of world-components: space, time, and objects. The most complete and suggestive classification of fictional worlds belongs to Martínez-Bonati (1983), who proposes four main distinctions: homogeneous versus heterogeneous, pure versus contaminated, realistic versus fantastic, and stable versus unstable. See also Doležel's (1984b) classification of Kafka's fictional worlds.

6. See, e.g., Fodor (1974). Putnam (1975b) discusses a principle of "local" relevance of explanation, leading to the idea of level-autonomy.

7. Nagel (1974) convincingly argued that a physicalist language cannot describe the phenomenal appearance of the universe as grasped from the point of view of a given species. See also Danto's similar argument (1984).

8. Notice that this situation is not reducible to dialectical logic. Although dialectical logic allows for contradictory predicates to be truthfully asserted about the same entity, negative theology directs its attention to cases in which contradictory predicates have to be used in order better to suggest the impossibility of adequate discourse.

9. Walton's 1978 papers present an early version of the theory; his 1980 paper, written for a public of literary specialists, leaves aside some of the more technical aspects. In 1984 he offers a condensed view of the theory. Evans (1982), pp. 343–372, develops an account of existential and nonexistential statements based on Walton's theory.

10. Eliade (1959), pp. 20–21. The authors quoted here concentrate upon phenomenological descriptions of the religious experience at the individual (Otto, 1923) or social levels (Weber, 1922; Caillois, 1959; Berger, 1967).

11. Among the rich literature on the subject, I should mention Cajetan's seventeenth-century treatise on the analogy of names (Vio, 1953).

12. In a series of recent papers, Doležel (1983, 1984) proposes illuminating readings of texts by Kafka and Hašek in terms of fictional-world semantics. See also Eco's classic paper (1979) devoted to a text by A. Allais.

13. See, e.g., chap. 72 of the second part, in which Quixote and Sancho meet Don Alvar Tarfé, a character in Avellaneda's book, who testifies to the irreconcilable difference between "his" (Avellaneda's) Quixote and the "real" (Cervantes') character.

## 4. Border, Distance, Size, Incompleteness

1. Modern aesthetics assumes that, rather than simply depicting their worlds, fictional texts create or establish them. My use of terms like "depicting" or "referring to" does not imply opposition to this stand; a text *depicts* or *refers to* its world in the sense that it gives us the necessary details about it. One can say, for instance, that Böcklin's painting depicts the Island of the Dead, without denying that it also creates or establishes it. But, I do not want to defend an unconditional "creative" stand either: in many cases texts take already existent worlds, be they real, mythological, or fictional, and simply add a few new touches. Creation is better used in a gradual rather than a discriminatory sense: texts more or less create their worlds.

2. See Ancel (1938), whose notions derive from the French school of "human geography."

3. Ehrlich (1955) translates the notion as "deautomatization"; see the discussion in Steiner's work on Russian formalism (1984), as well as Todorov's comments on the notion (1984).

4. See Lord (1960), Parry (1971), and Bäuml (1984). A different point of view, which insists on poetological principles and aesthetic effects in archaic poetry, has been defended by Sternberg (1978, 1983).

5. For an erudite study of eloquence in baroque literature, see Fumaroli (1980), who understands rhetoric less as an ensemble of formulaic patterns than as a flexible system for organizing the moral and literary contents.

6. Suleiman (1983) demonstrates how the authoritarian semantics of *romans à thèse* has important consequences on their structure. Her study suggests ways of correlating semantic and stylistic consideration of literary texts.

7. Walton (1980), p. 6; this paper represents a synthesis of two earlier contributions in 1978. The reasons why we are moved by the destiny of fictional beings have been thoroughly discussed by aestheticians; see Radford and Weston (1975), Paskins (1977), Skulsky (1980), Guthrie (1981). Shaper (1978) and Rosebury (1979) address the related topic of suspension of disbelief.

8. Cohn (1982) quotes Thomas Mann's revealing statement about the indirectness of writing, which allows the author to interpolate between himself and the reader a second voice: "wenn also . . . ein monsieur sich meldet und peroriert, der aber keineswegs identisch mit dem epischen Autor, sondern ein fingierten und schattenhafter Beobachter ist" (p. 223).

9. In addition to Frank (1963), see the issue of *Critical Inquiry*, 4 (Winter 1977), devoted to the topic, as well as Mitchell (1980).

10. Wolterstorff (1976), p. 125; further development of the theory in Wolterstorff (1980). For a penetrating review of the last item, see Walton (1983b).

11. Castañeda (1979), Howell (1979), and Routley (1979), among others.

## 5. Conventions

1. Thus Schmidt (1980, 1984) combines an empiricist and scientist literary theory with a radical conventionalism.

2. Saussure has always been an elusive figure. Early Swiss and French disciples (Bally, Meillet) developed the sociological and stylistic aspects of his teaching. Phonologists of the Prague school and American distributionalists paid tribute to his notion of linguistic system. Hjelmslev, and later Barthes, saw in Saussure the father of semiology. Derrida, Lacan, and the American poststructuralists attribute to him an anti-Aristotelian metaphysics of difference. For a balanced account of Saussure's ideas, see Culler (1976). Angenot (1984) offers a vivacious criticism of the use various theories have made of Saussure's name and ideas during the late sixties and early seventies. Eco's semiotics (1976, 1984) proves the possibility of constructing a synthesis between the Saussurian approach and the tradition of philosophy of language, analytical or not.

3. Although Hjelmslev's major linguistic contribution (1943) has been translated into English, his direct impact on American linguistics and semiotics remains minimal. Quite early, Chomsky's virulent criticism of structuralist models (1956, 1957) rendered obsolete the few attempts to study Hjelmslev's thought. It is only through French semiotics and structuralism that his name started to be mentioned again in the late sixties. A critical study of his contributions and influence is still much needed.

4. Barthes (1968b), Hamon (1973), Brooke-Rose (1980); Pavel (1985a) criticizes the conventionalist theory of realism. Brinker's important paper (1983) strongly argues against radical conventionalism. See, in the same vein, Hirsch's attack on conventionalism (1983).

5. Notably in Chomsky (1975, 1980). Piatelli-Palmarini (1980) provides the best collection of papers on the debate between constructivist and innatist theories of language learning. On pp. 287–309, Putnam's paper (1980) offers a devastating criticism of radical innatist arguments.

6. A history of the notion between 1500 and 1750 is provided by Manley (1970). See also Reeves (1982).

7. Herrnstein Smith (1978), pp. 24–40. An important study of conventions of reading, containing a theoretical introduction and precious bibliographical indications, is Mailloux (1982).

8.  To simplify the example, I use the two-level accent system, although representations can be devised to include several types of stress. The distinction between meter and rhythm employed here derives from Jakobson's theory (1960), which defines rhythmic pleasure as consisting in frustrated metric expectations. In the light of a Lewisian analysis, I would add *expected* frustrated expectations, since the metrical scheme provides a framework within which the coordination equilibrium is defined.

9.  A subtle discussion of genres as reading strategies can be found in Rabinowitz (1985). The interpretive conventions in Fish's sense (1982) are the object of Mailloux's study (1982); he distinguishes among traditional, regulative, and constitutive conventions. An earlier paper by Rabinowitz (1980) describes the various kinds of audience posited by texts of fiction; his suggestive classification can be read as a typology of the coordination games between writer and public.

10.  Should one include thematic studies here? Nussbaum's paper on Plato's and Proust's fictional thematization of the soul suggests that fictional hypotheses can be more than mere pre-conventional games (1983).

## 6. The Economy of the Imaginary

1.  For a presentation based on Schutz's paper on multiple realities (1962), see Berger's analysis (1970) of Musil's *The Man Without Qualities*. Bakhtin's notion (1981) of Chronotope comes surprisingly close to Schutz's views.

2.  Berger, Berger, and Kellner (1973) propose a phenomenological description of modern man's difficulties in stabilizing his ontological environment.

3.  There are more options available, to be sure: tolerant moralists might hold that there is a plurality of equally acceptable world models, but others that are definitely unacceptable; sophisticated relativists could claim that there are no absolutely right or wrong ones, but degrees of acceptablity or plausibility; utopian thinkers might hope that there is a single best and most acceptable world that is different from ones accepted in the past. (I owe this remark to Kendall Walton.)

4.  My proposals benefit from recent functionalist theories in the philosophy of psychology, especially from Putnam's articles, "Minds and Machines" (1960) and "The Nature of Mental States" (1967). An anthology of functionalism, accompanied by a critical presentation, can be found in Block (1981). Margolis (1984) discusses functionalism within the context of contemporary philosophy of psychology. Hofstadter and Dennet (1981) offer an instructive and amusing anthology, with annotated bibliography.

5.  For a discussion of the proposition theory, see Hospers (1946), chap. 5, and Beardsley (1981), chap. 8.

# References

Aarne, Antti, and Stith Thompson. 1961. *The Types of Folktales: A Classification and Bibliography*. Helsinki: Academia Scientiarum Fennica.

Ancel, Jacques. 1938. *Géographie des frontières*. Paris: Gallimard.

Angenot, Marc. 1984. "Structuralism as Syncretism: Institutional Distorsions of Saussure." in John Fekete, ed., *The Structural Allegory: Reconstructive Encounters with the New French Thought*. Minneapolis: University of Minnesota Press.

Aristotle. *The Poetics,* trans. and ed. L. J. Potts. Cambridge, Eng.: Cambridge University Press, 1968.

Austin, J. L. 1960. *How To Do Things with Words*. Cambridge: Harvard University Press.

Bakhtin, Mihail. 1981. *The Dialogic Imagination,* ed. M. Holquist, trans. C. Emerson and M. Holquist. Austin: University of Texas Press.

Banfield, Ann. 1982. *Unspeakable Sentences: Narration and Representation in the Language of Fiction*. London: Routledge.

Barthes, Roland. 1963. *Sur Racine*. Paris: Seuil.

——— 1966. "Introduction to the Structural Analysis of Narratives." in *Image, Music, Text,* trans. S. Heath. New York: Hill and Wang, 1977.

——— 1968a. "The Effect of Reality." In *French Literary Criticism Today,* ed. T. Todorov. Cambridge, Eng.: Cambridge University Press. 1982.

——— 1968b. "The Death of the Author." In *Image, Music, Text,* trans. S. Heath. New York: Hill and Wang, 1977.

Bauml, Franz H. 1984. "Medieval Texts and the Two Theories of Oral-Formulaic Composition: A Proposal for a Third Theory." *New Literary History,* 16:31–49.

Béguin, Albert. 1947. *Balzac visionnaire*. Geneva: Skira.

Beardsley, Monroe. 1981. *Aesthetics: Problems in the Philosophy of Criticism,* 2nd ed. Indianapolis: Hackett.

Berger, Peter. 1967. *The Sacred Canopy: Elements of a Sociological Theory of Religion*. Garden City: Doubleday.

———— 1970. "The Problem of Multiple Realities: Alfred Schutz and Robert Musil." In *Phenomenology and Social Reality*, ed. M. Natanson. Evanston: Northwestern University Press.

———— B. Berger, and H. Kellner. 1973. *The Homeless Mind: Modernization and Consciousness*. New York: Random House.

Block, Ned, ed. 1981. *Readings in the Philosophy of Psychology*, vol. 1. Cambridge: Harvard University Press.

Blocker, Gene. 1974. "The Truth about Fictional Entities." *Philosophical Quarterly*, 24:27–36.

Booth, Wayne. 1961. *The Rhetoric of Fiction*. Chicago: University of Chicago Press.

Bremond, Claude. 1973. *Logique du récit*. Paris: Seuil.

———— 1982. "Semiotique d'un conte mauricien." *Recherches sémiotiques/Semiotic Inquiry*, 2:405–423.

———— and J. Verrier. 1981. "Afanasiev and Propp," trans. T. Pavel and M. Randall. *Style*, 18 (1984):177–195.

Brinker, Menahem. 1983. "Verisimilitude, Conventions, and Belief." *New Literary History*, 14:253–267.

Brooke-Rose, Christine. 1980. "The Evil Ring: Realism and the Marvelous." *Poetics Today*, 1.4:67–90.

Brooks, Peter. 1984. *Reading for the Plot*. New York: Knopf.

Caillois, Roger. 1950. *Man and the Sacred*, trans. Meyer Barash. Glencoe: Free Press, 1959.

Castañeda, Hector-Neri. 1979. "Fiction and Reality: Their Fundamental Connections." *Poetics*, 8:31–62.

Chatman, Seymour. 1978. *Story and Discourse*. Ithaca: Cornell University Press.

Chisholm, R. M. 1973. "Homeless Objects." *Revue internationale de philosophie*, 104/5:207–223.

Chomsky, Noam. 1956. "Three Models of the Description of Language." In *I.R.E. Transactions on Informations Theory*, vol. IT-2.

———— 1957. *Syntactic Structures*. The Hague: Mouton.

———— 1965. *Current Issues in Linguistic Theory*. The Hague: Mouton.

———— 1975. *Reflections on Language*. New York: Pantheon.

———— 1980. "The Linguistic Approach." In *Language and Learning*, ed. M. Piatelli-Palmarini. Cambridge: Harvard University Press.

Cocchiarella, Nino. 1982. "Meinong Reconstructed versus Early Russell Reconstructed." *Journal of Philosophical Logic*, 11:183–214.

Cohn, Dorrit. 1978. *Transparent Minds: Narrative Modes for Presenting Consciousness in Fiction*. Princeton: Princeton University Press.

———— 1982. "The Second Author of 'Der Tod in Venedig.' " In *Probleme der Moderne: Studien zur deutschen Literatur von Nietzsche bis Brecht. Festschrift für Walter Sokel*, ed. B. Bennett, A. Kaes, and W. J. Lillyman. Tübingen: Niemeyer.

Creswell, M. J. 1972. "The World Is Everything That Is the Case." In *The Possible and the Actual*, ed. M. J. Loux. Ithaca: Cornell University Press, 1979.

Culler, Jonathan. 1975. *Structuralist Poetics*. Ithaca: Cornell University Press.

—— 1976. *Ferdinand de Saussure*. London: Fontana.

—— 1982. *On Deconstruction: Theory and Criticism after Structuralism*. Ithaca: Cornell University Press.

Curtius, E. R. 1948. *European Literature and the Latin Middle Ages*, trans. W. R. Trask. Princeton: Princeton University Press, 1953.

Csuri, K., ed. 1980. "Literary Semantics and Possible Worlds." *Studia Poetica*, 2.

Danto, Arthur C. 1964. "The Artworld." In *Philosophy Looks at the Arts*, ed. J. Margolis. Philadelphia: Temple University Press, 1978.

—— 1981. *The Transfiguration of the Commonplace: A Philosophy of Art*. Cambridge: Harvard University Press.

—— 1984. "Mind, Feeling, Form as Substance." *Journal of Philosophy*, 81:64–66.

DeBeaugrande, Robert. 1980. *Text, Discourse, and Process*. Norwood, N.J.: Ablex.

De Man, Paul. 1969. "The Rhetoric of Temporality." In *Blindness and Insight*, 2nd ed. Minneapolis: Minnesota University Press, 1983.

—— 1983. "The Resistance to Theory." *Yale French Studies*, 63:3–20.

Derrida, Jacques. 1967a. *Speech and Phenomena*, trans. D. Allison. Evanston: Northwestern University Press, 1973.

—— 1967b. *On Grammatology*, trans. G. S. Spivak. Baltimore: Johns Hopkins University Press, 1976.

—— 1977a. "Signature, Event, Context." *Glyph*, 1:172–197.

—— 1977b. "Limited Inc abc . . ." *Glyph*, 2:162–254.

Doležel, Lubomir. 1976a. "Narrative Modalities." *Journal of Literary Semantics*, 5.1:5–14.

—— 1976b. "Narrative Semantics." *PTL1*:129–51.

—— 1976c. "Narrative Worlds." In *Sound, Sign and Meaning*, ed. L. Matejka. Ann Arbor: Michigan Slavic Publications.

—— 1979. "Extensional and Intensional Narrative Worlds." *Poetics*, 8:193–212.

—— 1980. "Truth and Authenticity in Narrative." *Poetics Today*, 1.3:7–25.

—— 1983. "Intensional Function, Invisible Worlds, and Franz Kafka." *Style*, 17:120–141.

—— 1984a. "The Roads of History and the Detours of the Good Soldier." In *Language and Literary Theory. In Honor of Ladislav Matejka*, ed. B. Stolz, I. R. Titunik, and L. Doležel. Ann Arbor: Papers in Slavic Philosophy, V.

—— 1984b. "Kafka's Fictional Worlds." *Canadian Review of Comparative Literature*, 11:61–83.

Donnellan, Keith. 1966. "Reference and Definite Descriptions." *Philosophical Review*, 75:281–304.

—— 1974. "Speaking of Nothing." *Philosophical Review*, 83:3–32.

Dorfman, Eugene. 1969. *Narreme in the Medieval Romance Epic: An Introduction to Narrative Structures*. Toronto: University of Toronto Press.

Douglas, Mary. 1973. *Natural Symbols*. London: Barrie and Jenkins.

Eaton, Marcia. 1972. "The Truth Value of Literary Statements." *British Journal of Aesthetics*, 12:163–174.

Eco, Umberto. 1976. *A Theory of Semiotics*. Bloomington: Indiana University Press.

—— 1979. *"Lector in Fabula:* Pragmatic Strategy in a Metanarrative Text." In *The Role of the Reader: Explorations in the Semiotics of Texts*. Bloomington: Indiana University Press.

—— 1984. *Semiotics and the Philosophy of Language*. Bloomington: Indiana University Press.

Ehrlich, Victor. 1955. *Russian Formalism*. The Hague: Mouton.

Elgin, Catherine. 1983. *With Reference to Reference*. Indianapolis: Hackett.

Eliade, Mircea. 1955. "Littérature orale." In *Histoire des littératures*, I. *Encyclopédie de la Pléiade*. Paris: Gallimard.

—— 1957. *The Sacred and the Profane*. New York: Harper, 1959.

Eliot, T. S. 1957. *On Poetry and Poets*. London: Faber.

Evans, Gareth. 1973. "The Causal Theory of Names." *Aristotelian Society, Supplementary Volume*, 47:187–208.

—— 1982. *The Varieties of Reference*, ed. John McDowell. New York: Oxford University Press.

Fanto, James A. 1978. "Speech Act Theory and Its Applications to the Study of Literature." In *The Sign: Semiotics around the World*, ed. R. W. Bailey. L. Matejka, and P. Steiner. Ann Arbor: Michigan Slavic Publications.

Findlay, J. N. 1963. *Meinong's Theory of Objects and Values*. Oxford: Clarendon Press.

Fish, Stanley. 1976. "How To Do Things with Austin and Searle." *Modern Language Notes*, 91:983–1025.

—— 1982. *Is There a Text in This Class?* Cambridge: Harvard University Press.

Fodor, Jerry A. 1974. "Special Sciences, or the Disunity of Science as a Working Hypothesis." *Synthese*, 28:97–115.

Frank, Joseph. 1963. *The Widening Gyre*. New Brunswick: Rutgers University Press.

Frege, Gottlob. 1892. "On Sense and Reference." In *Philosophical Writings of Gottlob Frege*, ed. P. Geach and M. Black. Oxford: Blackwell, 1960.

Frye, Northrop. 1957. *Anatomy of Criticism*. Princeton: Princeton University Press.

Fumaroli, Marc. 1980. *L'Age de l'éloquence: Rhétorique et "res literaria" de la Renaissance au seuil de l'époque classique.* Geneva: Droz.

Gabriel, Gottfried. 1979. "Fiction—A Semantic Approach." *Poetics*, 8:245–255.

Gale, Richard M. 1971. "The Fictive Use of Language." *Philosophy*, 66:324–340.

Genette, Gérard. 1972. *Narrative Discourse: An Essay in Method,* trans. J. E. Lewin. Ithaca: Cornell University Press, 1980.

———— 1982. *Palimpsestes.* Paris: Seuil.

———— 1983. *Nouveau discours du récit.* Paris: Seuil.

Godzich, Wlad. 1983. "The Domestication of Derrida." In *The Yale Critics: Deconstruction in America,* ed. J. Arac, W. Godzich, and W. Martin. Minneapolis: University of Minnesota Press.

Goodman, Nelson. 1968. *Languages of Art.* Indianapolis: Bobbs-Merrill.

———— 1978. *Ways of Worldmaking.* Indianapolis: Hackett.

———— 1984. *Of Mind and Other Matters.* Cambridge: Harvard University Press.

Graff, Gerald. 1979. *Literature Against Itself: Literary Ideas in Modern Society.* Chicago: University of Chicago Press.

Greimas, A. J. 1970. *Du sens.* Paris: Seuil.

———— and J. Courtés. 1982. *Semiotics and Language: An Analytical Dictionary,* trans. L. Crist, D. Patte, et al. Bloomington: Indiana University Press.

Grice, H. Paul. 1975. "Logic and Conversation." In *Speech Acts (Syntax and Semantics, 3),* ed. P. Cole and J. L. Morgan. New York: Academic Press.

Guthrie, Jerry. 1981. "Self-Description and Emotional Response to Fiction." *British Journal of Aesthetics,* 21:45–67.

Hamon, Philippe. 1973. "Un discours contraint." In *Littérature et réalité,* ed. R. Barthes et al. Paris: Seuil, 1982.

Hartman, Geoffrey. 1980. *Criticism in the Wilderness: The Study of Literature Today.* New Haven: Yale University Press.

Herrnstein Smith, Barbara 1978. *On the Margins of Discourse.* Chicago: University of Chicago Press.

Hintikka, Jaako. 1963. "The Modes of Modality." *Acta Philosphia Fennica,* 16:65–79.

Hirsch, E. D., Jr. 1983. "Beyond Convention." *New Literary History,* 14:389–397.

Hjelmslev, Louis. 1943. *Prolegomena to a Theory of Language,* trans. F. J. Whitfield. Madison: University of Wisconsin Press, 1963.

Hofstadter, D. R., and D. C. Dennett. 1981. *The Mind's I.* New York: Bantam.

Hospers, John. 1946. *Meaning and Truth in the Arts.* Chapel Hill: University of North Carolina Press.

Howell, Robert. 1979. "Fictional Objects: How They Are and How They Aren't." *Poetics,* 8:129–178.

Hrushovski, Benjamin. 1979. "The Structure of Semiotic Objects: A Three-Dimensional Model." *Poetics Today*, 1. 1–2:363–376.

—— 1984a. "Poetic Metaphor and Frames of Reference." *Poetics Today*, 5.1:5–43.

—— 1984b. "Fictionality and Fields of Reference." *Poetics Today*, 5.2:227–51.

Ihwe, Jens, and H. Rieser. 1979. "Normative and Descriptive Theory of Fiction: Some Contemporary Issues." *Poetics*, 8:63–84.

Ingarden, Roman. 1965. *The Literary Work of Art*, trans. G. Grabowicz. Evanston: Northwestern University Press.

Inwagen, Peter van. 1977. "Creatures of Fiction." *American Philosophical Quarterly*, 14:99–308.

Jakobson, Roman. 1960. "Linguistics and Poetics." In *Style in Language*, ed. T. A. Sebeok. Cambridge: MIT Press.

Kaplan, David. 1968. "Qantifying In." *Synthèse*, 19:178–214.

Kirk, G. S. 1970. *Myth: Its Meaning and Function in Ancient and Other Cultures*. Cambridge, Eng.: Cambridge University Press.

Körner, Stephen. 1973. "Individuals in Possible Worlds." In *Logic and Ontology*, ed. M. K. Munitz. New York: New York University Press.

Kripke, Saul. 1963. "Semantical Considerations on Modal Logic." *Acta Philosophica Fennica*, 16:83–94.

—— 1972a. "Naming and Necessity." In *Semantics of Natural Language*, ed. D. Davidson and G. Harman. Dordrecht: Reidel.

—— 1972b. "Existence: Vacuous Names and Mythical Kinds." Unpublished paper.

—— 1979. "Speaker's Reference and Semantic Reference." In *Contemporary Perspectives in the Philosophy of Language*, ed. P. A. French, T. E. Uehling, Jr., and H. W. Wettstein. Minneapolis: University of Minnesota Press.

Lambert, Karel. 1974. "Impossible Objects." *Inquiry*, 17:303–334.

—— 1976. "On the Durability of Impossible Objects." *Inquiry*, 19:251–253.

—— 1983. *Meinong and the Principle of Independence*. Cambridge, Eng.: Cambridge University Press.

Lebowitz, Michael. 1984. "Creating Characters in a Story-Telling Universe." *Poetics*, 13:171–194.

Le Goff, Jacques. 1981. *La Naissance du purgatoire*. Paris: Gallimard.

Levi-Strauss, Claude. 1960. "L'Analyse morphologique des contes russes." *International Journal of Slavic Linguistics and Poetics*, 3:122–149.

—— 1963. *Structural Anthropology*, trans. C. Jakobson and B. Grundfest Schoepf. New York: Harper.

Lewis, David. 1969. *Convention*. Cambridge: Harvard University Press.

—— 1970. "Anselm and Actuality." *Nous*, 4:175–88.

—— 1973. *Counterfactuals*. Cambridge: Harvard University Press.

—— 1978. "Truth in Fiction." *American Philosophical Quarterly*, 15:37–46.

Lewis, Philip. 1982. "The Post-Structuralist Condition." *Diacritics*, 12. 1:1–24.

Linsky, Leonard. 1977. *Names and Descriptions*. Chicago: University of Chicago Press.

Lord, Albert B. 1960. *The Singer of Tales*. Cambridge: Harvard University Press.

Loux, Michael J., ed. 1979. *The Possible and the Actual: Readings in the Metaphysics of Modality*. Ithaca: Cornell University Press.

Mailloux, Steven. 1982. *Interpretive Conventions: The Reader in the Study of American Fiction*. Ithaca: Cornell University Press.

Malcolm, Norman. 1951. "Knowledge and Belief." In *Knowledge and Belief*, ed. A. Phillips Griffiths. London: Oxford University Press, 1967.

Manley, Lawrence. 1980. *Convention, 1500–1700*. Cambridge: Harvard University Press.

Margolis, Joseph. 1963. *The Language of Art and Art Criticism*. Detroit: Wayne State University Press.

——— 1977. "The Ontological Peculiarity of Works of Art." *Journal of Aesthetics and Art Criticism*, 36:45–50.

——— 1979. "Literature and Speech Acts." *Philosophy and Literature*, 3:39–52.

——— 1980. *Art and Philosophy*. Atlantic Highlands: Humanities.

——— 1983. "The Logic and Structure of Fictional Narratives." *Philosophy and Literature*, 7:162–181.

——— 1984. *Philosophy of Psychology*. Englewood Cliffs: Prentice Hall.

Martin, Wallace. 1983. Introduction to J. Arac, W. Godzich, and W. Martin, eds., *The Yale Critics: Deconstruction in America*. Minneapolis: University of Minnesota Press.

Martínez-Bonati, Felix. 1981. *Fictive Discourse and the Structure of Literature*. Ithaca: Cornell University Press.

——— 1983. "Towards a Formal Ontology of Fictional Worlds." *Philosophy and Literature*, 7:182–195.

Meinong, Alexis. 1904. "On the Theory of Objects." In *Realism and the Background of Phenomenlogy*, ed. R. M. Chisholm. New York: Free Press, 1960.

Miller, J. Hillis. 1980. "A Guest in the House: Reply to Shlomith Rimmon-Kenan's Reply." *Poetics Today*, 2.1b:189–191.

Mitchell, W. J. T. 1980. "Spatial Form in Literature: Toward a General Theory." *Critical Inquiry*, 6:539–567.

Moore, G. E. 1933. "Imaginary Objects." *Aristotelian Society, Supplementary Volume*, 12:55–70.

Nagel, Thomas. 1974. "What Is It Like To Be a Bat?" *Philosophical Review*, 83:435–450.

Nussbaum, Martha. 1983. "Fictions of the Soul." *Philosophy and Literature*, 7:145–161.

Ogden, C. K. 1932. *Bentham's Theory of Fictions.* Patterson: Littlefield, 1959.

—— and I. A. Richards. 1923. *The Meaning of Meaning.* New York: Harcourt.

Ohmann, Richard. 1971. "Speech Acts and the Definition of Literature." *Philosophy and Rhetoric,* 4:1–19.

—— 1972. "Instrumental Style: Notes on the Theory of Speech as Action." In *Current Trends in Stylistics,* ed. B. B. Kachru and F. W. Stahlke. Edmonton: Linguistic Research.

Ong, Walter J. 1981. *Orality and Literacy: The Technologizing of the Word.* London: Methuen.

Otto, Rudolf. 1923. *The Sacred,* trans. J. W. Harvey. London: Oxford University Press.

Parry, Adam, ed. 1971. *Making of Homeric Verse: Collected Papers of Milman Parry.* London: Oxford University Press.

Parsons, Terence. 1980. *Nonexistent Objects.* New Haven: Yale University Press.

Paskins, Barrie. 1977. "On Being Moved by Anna Karenina and *Anna Karenina.*" *Philosophy,* 52:344–347.

Pavel, Thomas G. 1976. *La Syntaxe narrative des tragédies de Corneille.* Paris: Klincksieck.

—— 1979. "Phonology and Myth-Analysis." In *Text vs. Sentence,* vol. 2, ed. J. Petöfi. Hamburg: Buske.

—— 1980. "Le Sel de la terre." *Revue de métaphysique et de morale,* 85:539–542.

—— 1982. "Plot-Structure and Style: Remarks on an Unstable Relationship." *Canadian Review of Comparative Literature,* 9:27–45.

—— 1985a. "Convention et représentation." *Littérature,* 57:31–47.

—— 1985b. *The Poetics of Plot: The Case of English Renaissance Drama.* Minneapolis: University of Minnesota Press.

Piatelli-Palmarini, M., ed. 1980. *Language and Learning. The Debate Between Piaget and Noam Chomsky.* Cambridge: Harvard University Press.

Plantinga, Alvin. 1974. *The Nature of Necessity.* Oxford: Clarendon Press.

—— 1976. "Actualism and Possible Worlds." *Theoria,* 42:139–160.

Polanyi, Michel. 1958. *Personal Knowledge: Towards a Post-Critical Philosophy.* Chicago: University of Chicago Press.

Pratt, Mary-Louise. 1977. *Toward a Speech Act Theory of Literary Discourse.* Bloomington: Indiana University Press.

Price, H. H. 1934–35. "Some Considerations about Belief." In *Knowledge and Belief,* ed. A. Phillips Griffiths. London: Oxford University Press, 1967.

Prince, Gerald. 1973. *A Grammar of Stories.* The Hague: Mouton.

—— 1982. *Narratology.* The Hague: Mouton.

—— 1983. "Worlds with Style." *Philosophy and Literature,* 7:78–88.

Propp, Vladimir. 1928. *Morphology of the Folktale,* trans. L. Scott, rev. Louis A. Wagner. Austin: University of Texas Press. 1968.

——— 1946. *Les Racines historiques du conte merveilleux,* trans. L. Gruel-Apert. Paris: Gallimard, 1983. English trans. of two chaps. in V. Propp, *Theory and History of Folklore,* trans. A. Y. Martin and R. P. Martin. Minneapolis: University of Minnesota Press, 1984.

——— 1966. "Study of the Folktale: Structure and History." *Dispositio,* 1(1976):277–92.

Putnam, Hilary. 1960. "Minds and Machines." Reprinted in *Mind, Language and Reality: Philosophical Papers,* vol. 2. Cambridge, Eng.: Cambridge University Press, 1975.

——— 1965. "How Not To Talk about Meaning." In *Mind, Language and Reality.*

——— 1967. "The Nature of Mental States." in *Mind, Language and Reality.*

——— 1970. "Is Semantics Possible?" In *Mind, Language and Reality.*

——— 1973. "Meaning and Reference." *Journal of Philosophy,* 70:699–711.

——— 1975. "The Meaning of 'Meaning.' " In *Mind, Language and Reality.*

——— 1980. "What Is Innate and Why: Comments on the Debate." In *Language and Learning,* ed. M. Piatelli-Palmarini. Cambridge: Harvard University Press.

——— 1983. "Is There a Fact of Matter About Fiction?" *Poetics Today,* 4.1:77–82.

——— 1984. "The Craving for Objectivity." *New Literary History,* 15:229–239.

Quine, Willard V. 1936. "Truth by Convention." In *Philosophical Essays for A. N. Whitehead,* ed. O. H. Lee. New York: Longmans.

——— 1969. *Ontological Relativity and Other Essays.* New York: Columbia University Press.

Rabinowitz, Peter J. 1980. " 'What's Hecuba to Us?' The Audience's Experience of Literary Borrowing" In *The Reader in the Text: Essays on Audience and Interpretation,* ed. S. Suleiman and I. Crosman. Princeton: Princeton University Press.

——— 1985. "The Turn of the Glass Key: Popular Fiction as Reading Strategy." *Critical Inquiry,* 11:418–431.

Radford, Colin, and M. Weston. 1975. "How Can We Be Moved by the Fate of Anna Karenina?" *Aristotelian Society, Supplementary Volume,* 49:67–93.

Reeves, Charles Eric. 1982. "Convention and Literary Behaviour." In *The Structure of Literary Process. Studies Dedicated to the Memory of Felix Vodicka,* ed. P. Steiner, M. Cervenka, and R. Vroom. Amsterdam: Benjamins.

Rescher, N. 1976. "The Ontology of the Possible." In *Logic and Ontology,* ed. M. Munitz. New York: New York University Press.

Richards, I. A. 1925. *Principles of Literary Criticism*. New York: Harcourt.

Ricoeur, Paul. 1982. *Temps et récit*. Paris: Seuil. English trans., *Time and Narrative*. Chicago: University of Chicago Press, 1984.

—— 1984. *La Configuration dans le récit de fiction (Temps et récit, 2)*. Paris: Seuil.

Rieser, Hannes, ed. 1982. "Semantics of Fiction." *Poetics*, 11:63–84.

Riffaterre, Michael. 1978a. *Semiotics of Poetry*. Bloomington: Indiana University Press.

—— 1978b. "L'Illusion référentielle." In *Littérature et réalité*, ed. R. Barthes et al. Paris: Seuil, 1980.

Rimmon-Kenan, Shlomith. 1980. "Deconstructive Reflections on Deconstruction." *Poetics Today*, 2.1b:185–188.

—— 1983. *Narrative Fiction: Contemporary Poetics*. London: Methuen.

Rorty, Richard. 1979. "Is There a Problem about Fictional Discourse?" In *Consequences of Pragmatism (Essays, 1972–1980)*. Minneapolis: University of Minnesota Press, 1982.

Rosebury, B. J. 1979. "Fiction, Emotion and 'Belief': A Reply to Eva Schaper." *British Journal of Aesthetics*, 19:120–130.

Rougemont, Denis de. 1939. *Love in the Western World*, trans. M. Belgion. New York: Harper, 1974.

Routley, Richard. 1979. "The Semantical Structures of Fictional Discourse." *Poetics*, 8:3–30.

—— 1980. *Exploring Meinong's Jungle*. Canberra: Philosophy Department, Australian National University, Monograph 3.

Russell, Bertrand. 1905a. Review of A. Meinong's *Untersuchungen zur Gegenstandstheorie und Psychologie*. *Mind*, 14:530–538.

—— 1905b. "On Denoting." In *Logic and Knowledge*, ed. R. C. Marsh. London: Allen and Unwin.

—— 1957. "Mr. Strawson on Referring." *Mind*, 66:385–389.

Ryan, Marie-Laure. 1980. "Fiction, Non-Factuals and the Principle of Minimal Departure." *Poetics*, 8:403–422.

—— 1984. "Fictions as a Logical, Ontological, and Illocutionary Issue." *Style*, 18:121–139.

—— Forthcoming. "The Modal Structure of Narrative Universes." *Poetics Today*.

Ryle, Gilbert. 1933. "Imaginary Objects." *Aristotelian Society, Supplementary Volume*, 12:18–43.

Schaper, Eva. 1978. "Fiction and the Suspension of Disbelief." *British Journal of Aesthetics*, 18:31–44.

Saussure, Ferdinand de. 1916. *Course in General Linguistics*, trans. W. Baskin. New York: McGraw-Hill, 1966.

Schmidt, Siegfried J. 1980. "Fictionality in Literary and Non-Literary Discourse." *Poetics*, 9:525–546.

—— 1984. "The Fiction Is That Reality Exists." *Poetics Today*, 5.2(1984):253–274.

Scholes, Robert. 1984. *Structuralism in Literature*. New Haven: Yale University Press.

Schutz, A. 1962. "On Multiple Realities." In *Collected Papers*, vol. 1. The Hague: Nijhoff.

Schwartz, Stephen P., ed. 1977. *Naming, Necessity and Natural Kinds*. Ithaca: Cornell University Press.

Searle, John. 1958. "On Proper Names." *Mind*, 67:166–173.

—— 1969. *Speech Acts*. London: Cambridge University Press.

—— 1975a. "Indirect Speech Acts." In *Speech Acts (Syntax and Semantics, 3)*, ed. P. Cole and J. L. Morgan. New York: Academic Press.

—— 1975b. "The Logical Status of Fictional Discourse." *New Literary History*, 6:319–332.

—— 1979. "Metaphor." In *Metaphor and Thought*, ed. A. Ortony. London: Cambridge University Press.

Shank, R. C., and R. P. Abelson. 1977. *Scripts, Plans, Goals, and Understanding*. Hillsdale: Erlbaum.

Sibley, Frank. 1959. "Aesthetic Concepts." *Philosophical Review*, 68:421–450.

Skulsky, Harold. 1980. "On Being Moved by Fiction." *Journal of Aesthetics and Art Criticism*, 39:5–14.

Sora, Michel. 1947. *Du Dialogue intérieur: Fragment d'une anthropologie métaphysique*. Paris: Gallimard.

—— 1978. *Sarea pamîntului*. Bucharest: Cartea Romaneasca.

Sparshott, F. E. 1967. "Truth in Fiction." *Journal of Aesthetics and Art Criticism*, 26:3–7.

Stalnaker, Robert C. 1976. "Possible Worlds." *Nous*, 10:65–75.

Steiner, Peter. 1984. *Russian Formalism: A Metapoetics*. Ithaca: Cornell University Press.

Sternberg, Meir. 1978. *Expositional Modes and Temporal Ordering in Fiction*. Baltimore: John Hopkins University Press.

—— 1983. "The Bible's Art of Persuasion: Ideology, Rhetoric and Poetics in Saul's Fall." *Hebrew Union College Annual*, 54:45–82.

Stoll, E. E. 1933. *Art and Artifice in Shakespeare*. Cambridge, Eng.: Cambridge University Press.

Strawson, P. F. 1956. "On Referring." In *Essays in a Conceptual Analysis*, ed. A. Flew. Houndmills Basingstoke: Macmillan.

—— 1964. "Identifying Reference and Truth-Value." *Theoria*, 30:96–118.

Suleiman, Susan. 1980. Introduction to S. Suleiman and I. Crosman, eds., *The Reader in the Text: Essays on Audience and Interpretation*. Princeton: Princeton University Press.

—— 1983. *Authoritarian Fictions: The Ideological Novel as a Literary Genre*. New York: Columbia University Press.

Summers, M., ed. 1966. *Shakespearian Adaptations*. New York: Haskel.

Thibaudet, Albert. 1936. *Histoire de la littérature française de 1789 à nos jours*. Paris: Stock.

Todorov, Tzvetan. 1968. *An Introduction to Poetics*, trans. R. Howard. Minneapolis: Minnesota University Press, 1981.

——— 1971. *The Poetics of Prose*, trans. R. Howard. Ithaca: Cornell University Press.

——— 1977. *Les Genres du discours*. Paris: Seuil.

——— 1984. "Le Langage poétique (Les Formalistes russes)." In *Critique de la critique*. Paris: Seuil.

Tompkins, Jane P. 1980. Introduction to J. Tompkins, ed., *Reader-Response Criticism*. Baltimore: Johns Hopkins University Press.

Turner, Victor. 1980. "Social Dramas and Stories about Them." In *On Narrative*, ed. W.J.T. Mitchell, Chicago: University of Chicago Press.

Vaihinger, Hans. 1911. *The Philosophy of "As If,"* trans. C. K. Ogden, 2nd ed. London: Routledge, 1965.

*Versus*, 17. 1977. *Théorie des mondes possibles et sémiotique textuelle*.

*Versus*, 19/20. 1978. *Semiotica testuale: Mondi possibili e narratività*.

Vio, Tommaso de [Cajetan]. *The Analogy of Names and the Concept of Being*, trans. E. A. Bushinski and H. J. Koren. Pittsburgh: Duquesne University Press, 1953.

Von Wright, G. H. 1966. "The Logic of Action—A Sketch." In *The Logic of Decision and Action*, ed. N. Rescher. Pittsburgh: University of Pittsburgh Press.

Walton, Kendall. 1970. "Categories of Art." *Philosophical Review*, 79:334–367.

——— 1978a. "How Remote Are Fictional Worlds from the Real World?" *Journal of Aesthetics and Art Criticism*, 37:11–23.

——— 1978b. "Fearing Fictions." *Journal of Philosophy*, 75:5–27.

——— 1980. "Appreciating Fiction: Suspending Disbelief or Pretending Belief?" *Dispositio*, 5.13–14:1–18.

——— 1983a. "Fiction, Fiction-Making and Styles of Fictionality." *Philosophy and Literature*, 7:78–88.

——— 1983b. Review of N. Wolterstorff, *Works and Worlds of Art. Journal of Philosophy*, 80:179–183.

——— 1984. "Do We Need Fictional Entities? Notes Toward a Theory." In *Aesthetics: Proceedings of the Eighth International Wittgenstein Symposium*. Vienna: Hölder-Pichler-Temsky.

Weber, Max. 1922. *The Sociology of Religion*, trans. E. Fishoff. Boston: Beacon Press, 1963.

Weitz, Morris. 1956. "The Role of Theory in Aesthetics." In *Philosophy Looks at the Arts*, ed. J. Margolis. Philadelphia: Temple University Press, 1978.

White, Alan R. 1957. "On Claiming to Know." In *Knowledge and Belief*, ed. A. Phillips Griffiths. London: Oxford University Press, 1967.

Williams, Bernard. 1968. "Imagination and the Self." In *Studies in the Philosophy of Thought and Action*, ed.P. F. Strawson. New York: Oxford University Press.

Wimsatt, W. K., Jr., and M. C. Beardsley. 1949. "The Affective Fallacy." *Sewanee Review*, 57:458–488.

Winner, Ellen. 1982. *Invented Worlds: The Psychology of the Arts*. Cambridge: Harvard University Press.

Wittgenstein, Ludwig von. 1918. *Tractatus Logico-Philosophicus*, trans. D. F.Pears and B. F. McGuinness. London: Routledge.

—— 1953. *Philosophical Investigations*. New York: Macmillan.

Wolterstorff, Nicholas. 1976. "Worlds of Works of Art." *Journal of Aesthetics and Art Criticism*, 35:121–132.

—— 1980. *Worlds and Works of Art*. New York: Oxford University Press.

Woods, John. 1974. *The Logic of Fiction*. The Hague: Mouton.

—— 1982. "Animadversions and Open Questions, Reference, Inference and Truth in Fiction." *Poetics*, 11:553–562.

—— and T. G. Pavel, eds. 1979. "Formal Semantics and Literary Theory." *Poetics*, 8:1–268.

Woozley, A. D. 1952–53. "Knowing and Not Knowing." In *Knowledge and Belief*, ed. A. Phillips Griffiths. London: Oxford University Press, 1967.

Zumthor, Paul. 1983. *Introduction à la poésie orale*. Paris: Seuil.

# Index